CIVILIZATION
AND ITS
DISCONTENTS

First Warbler Press Edition 2022

Civilization and Its Discontents first published in 1930 as *Das Unbehagen in der Kultur* by Internationaler Psychoanalytischer Verlag, Vienna, Austria.

Translation © 2022 Ulrich Baer

"Freud: The Psycho-archeology of Civilizations" by Carl E. Schorske first published in *Proceedings of the Massachusetts Historical Society,* 1980, Third Series, Vol. 92, Massachusetts Historical Society, 1980, 52-67. Reprinted with permission of Massachusetts Historical Society.

"Freud and Moral Reflection" by Richard Rorty first published in *Pragmatism's Freud: The Moral Disposition of Psychoanalysis,* eds. Joseph H. Smith, M.D., and William Kerrigan, 1-27. © 1986 Forum on Psychiatry and the Humanities. Reprinted with permission of Johns Hopkins University Press.

ISBN 978-1-957240-58-9 (paperback)
ISBN 978-1-957240-59-6 (e-book)

warblerpress.com

Printed in the United States of America. This edition is printed with chlorine-free ink on acid-free interior paper made from 30% post-consumer waste recycled material.

CIVILIZATION
AND ITS
DISCONTENTS

SIGMUND FREUD

TRANSLATED BY ULRICH BAER
WITH ESSAYS BY CARL E. SCHORSKE
AND RICHARD RORTY

CONTENTS

I

One cannot help but get the impression that people generally measure
with incorrect standards, strive for power, success, and wealth for
themselves and admire them in others, but underestimate the true
values of life. And yet with each such general judgment one is in danger of
forgetting the colorful diversity of the human world and its spiritual life.
There are individuals who are not denied the admiration of their contemporaries, although their greatness is based on qualities and achievements
that are quite alien to the goals and ideals of the crowd. It is easy to assume
that it is only a minority who recognizes these great men, while the great
majority does not want to know anything about them. But things are probably not as simple as that, thanks to the inconsistencies between people's
thinking and actions and the diversity of their desires.

One of these excellent men calls himself my friend in our correspon-
dence. I had sent him my little pamphlet, which treats of religion as an
illusion, and he replied that he completely agreed with my judgment on
religion but regretted that I had not appreciated the actual source of religi-
osity.[1] He described it as a special feeling that never leaves him, that he has
found confirmed by many others, and that he can assume to exist for mil-
lions of people. A feeling that he would like to call the feeling of "eternity,"
a feeling of something seemingly unlimited, limitless, as it were, "oceanic."
This feeling is a purely subjective fact and not a matter of belief, according
to him; it involves no assurance of personal continuity but is the source
of religious energy that is captured by the various churches and religious
systems, directed into specific channels and surely also exhausted by them.

---

1   [Freud, *The Future of an Illusion* (1927). All notes and comments in brackets
are added by the translator.]

Only because of this oceanic feeling should one call oneself religious, even if one rejects every belief and every illusion.

This statement by my honored friend, who himself once paid poetic tribute to the magic of illusion, caused me considerable difficulties.[2] I myself cannot discover this oceanic feeling in myself. It is not convenient to work on feelings scientifically. One can try to describe their physiological symptoms. Where this is not feasible—and I fear that the oceanic feeling will also elude such an account—there remains no other option but to stick to the imagined content that is most likely to be associated with the feeling. If I have understood my friend correctly, he means the same thing that an original and quite peculiar poet gives to his protagonist as consolation before a freely chosen death: "We will not fall out of this world."[3] There exists a feeling of indissoluble connection and belonging with the entirety of the exterior world. To me, this has something of the character of an intellectual insight, certainly not without an accompanying emotional tone, as it will also be found in other mental efforts of similar scope. I could not convince myself in person of the primary nature of such a feeling. But that is no reason for me to deny its actual occurrence in others. The only question is whether it is correctly interpreted and whether it should be recognized as the "*fons et origo*" [source and origin] of every need for religion.

I have nothing to offer that would decisively influence the solution of this problem. The notion that man should receive information about his connection with the external world through an immediate feeling that has such an aim from the beginning sounds so strange and fits so poorly into the fabric of our psychology that we may attempt a psychoanalytic, i.e., genetic, derivation of such a feeling. We then have available to us the following train of thought: Normally nothing is more secure than the feeling of our self, of our own ego. This I, or ego, appears to us to be independent, uniform, well delimited from everything else. That this appearance is a deception, and that the ego in fact extends inward without any sharp boundary into our unconscious, mental being, which we call the id, for which it serves as a facade, as it were, is something psychoanalysis taught us, in addition to

2   After the publication of *La vie de Ramakrishna* (1929) and *La vie de Vivekananda* (1930) I no longer have to conceal that the friend alluded to here is Romain Rolland [1866–1944; French literary author and recipient of the 1915 Nobel Prize.]

3   C[hristian] D[ietrich] Grabbe, *Hannibal* (1835): "Indeed, we will not fall out of this world. We are in it, after all."

many other new details about the relation of the ego to the id. But toward the outside, at least, the ego seems to maintain clear and sharp boundaries. Only in one extraordinary state, but one that cannot be condemned as pathological, does it change. At the height of being in love, the line between self and object threatens to blur. Contrary to all evidence of the senses, the lover claims that "I" and "You" are one and is ready to behave as if it were so. What can be canceled temporarily by a physiological function, of course, must also be liable to be disturbed by pathological processes. Pathology provides insights into a great number of states in which the delimitation of the ego against the outside world becomes uncertain or the boundaries are really incorrectly drawn. These are cases in which parts of our own body, even pieces of our own mental life, perceptions, thoughts, or feelings appear as something strange that does not belong to the ego, as well as others in which one ascribes to the outside world what has evidently originated in the ego and should be recognized by it as such. It follows that the sense of the ego is also subject to disturbances, and the ego's boundaries are not permanent.

There is a further consideration: the adult's sense of self cannot have been this way from the beginning. It must have undergone a development which, understandably, cannot be proven, but which, with some probability, can be reconstructed.[4] The infant does not yet separate its ego from an external world as the source of the sensations flowing into it. He gradually learns this in response to various suggestions. It must make the strongest impression on him that some of the sources of excitation, in which he will later recognize his bodily organs, can send him sensations at any time, while others withdraw from him at times—including the most desirable: the mother's breast—and are only fetched by screaming for help. In this way the ego is first opposed by an "object," as something that is "outside" and is only forced into appearance through a special action. A further motivation to detach the ego from the mass of sensations and thus to recognize the "outside" of an external world is provided by the frequent, diverse, and inevitable sensations of pain and discomfort, which the unrestrictedly prevailing pleasure principle means to abolish and avoid. There arises then the tendency to separate everything that can become a source of such displeasure from the ego, to cast it outward, and to form a pure pleasure-ego confronted with a

---

4   See the numerous works on the development of the ego and feeling for the ego by [Sándor] Ferenczi, *Stages in the Development of the Sense of Reality* (1913), up to the contributions by P[aul] Federn 1926, 1927, and later.

strange, threatening outside. The boundaries of this primitive pleasure-ego cannot avoid being corrected by experience. Some things that you do not want to give up because they provide pleasure are not you, after all, but are separate objects, and some torment that you want to cast out turns out to be inseparable from the ego as its inner origin. We come to learn a procedure of how to differentiate between what is internal—belonging to the ego—and what is external—originating from the external world—through the deliberate control of our sensory activity and suitable muscular action. In doing so, we take the first step towards the establishment of the reality principle, which is to dominate further development. This distinction naturally serves the practical purpose of warding off both actually experienced and threatening feelings of discomfort. The fact that the ego uses methods to ward off certain internal displeasure that are not different from those it uses against external discomfort becomes the starting point for significant pathological disturbances.

In this way, then, the ego detaches itself from the outside world. To put it more correctly: originally the ego contains everything, and only later it separates an outside world from itself. Our sense of self today is only a shrunken remnant of a far more comprehensive and indeed all-encompassing feeling, which corresponded to a more intimate connection of the ego with the environment. If we can assume that this primary sense of self has been preserved in the mental life of many people to a greater or lesser extent, then it would be a kind of counterpart to the narrower and more sharply delimited sense of self during the period of maturity. The ideas that correspond to it would be exactly those of boundlessness and connection with the universe, and thus those which my friend used to explain the oceanic feeling. But do we have a right to assume that the original sensation survived alongside the later one into which it developed?

Without a doubt, for such an occurrence is strange neither in the mental nor in any other area. For the animal kingdom, we maintain the assumption that the most highly developed species evolved from the lowest. Yet we still find all simple forms of life among the living today. The group of the great dinosaurs has gone extinct and given way to mammals, but a real representative of this group, the crocodile, still lives with us. The analogy may be far-fetched, and it suffers from the fact that the surviving lower species are in most cases not really the ancestors of today's more highly developed ones. The intermediate links are usually extinct and only known through reconstruction. In the mental sphere, on the other hand, the preservation

of the primitive is so common alongside that into which it has transt
that it is unnecessary to prove it by examples. This occurrence is u.   -y
the result of a developmental split. One quantitative part of an attitude, of
an instinctual impulse, has remained unchanged, while another has undergone further development.

Here we touch upon the more general problem of preservation in the
psychic realm, which has hardly been dealt with but is so intriguing and
significant that we may pay attention to it for a while, even if the occasion
is insufficient. Since we have overcome the error that the familiar process of
forgetting means a destruction of the memory trace, i.e., annihilation, we
tend to the opposite assumption that nothing in mental life that had once
been formed can ever perish, that everything is somehow preserved and
can become manifest under suitable conditions, for example, by means of
a far-reaching regression. By way of a comparison to another area we can
try to clarify the meaning of this assumption. We take the development of
the Eternal City of Rome as an example.[5] Historians tell us that the oldest
Rome was the *Roma Quadrata*, a fenced settlement on the Palatine Hill.
Then followed the phase of the *Septimontium*, as a union of the settlements
on separate hills, then the city bounded by the Servian Wall, and even
later, after all the transformations of the republican and earlier imperial
times, the city that Emperor Aurelianus enclosed with his walls. We will not
pursue the transformations in the city any further but ask ourselves what a
visitor, whom we imagine to be equipped with the most perfect historical
and topographical knowledge, may still encounter in today's Rome from
these early stages. He will see the Aurelian Wall almost unchanged except
for a few gaps. In some places he can find stretches of the Servian Wall excavated. If he knows enough—more than today's archeologists—he might
be able to trace the entire course of this wall and the outline of the *Roma
Quadrata* into the cityscape. He finds little or nothing of the buildings that
once filled these old frames, because they no longer exist. The utmost he
can do with the best knowledge of the Rome of the republic would be to
know the original locations of the temples and public buildings of that time.
What now occupies these places are ruins, but not of the original struc-
tures but of rebuilt versions from later times after fires and destruction. It
hardly needs special mention that all these remains of ancient Rome appear

---

5   Based on *The Cambridge Ancient History*, VII (1928): "The Founding of Rome,"
by Hugh Last.

as scattered fragments in the tangle of a major metropolis from the more recent centuries after the Renaissance. Surely some old parts are still buried in the soil of the city or underneath its modern buildings. This is the kind of preservation of the past that we encounter in historical sites like Rome.

Now let us make the fantastic assumption that Rome is not a human dwelling but a psychic being with a similarly long and rich past, in which nothing that had once come about has perished, and in which, in addition to the most recent phase of development, all previous phases still exist. For Rome this would mean that on the Palatine Hill the imperial palaces and the Septizonium of Septimius Severus still rise to their old height, that the castle of Sant'Angelo still bears on its battlements the beautiful statues with which it was adorned until the siege of the Goths, etc. There is even more: at the place of the Palazzo Caffarelli would stand again the temple of Jupiter Capitolinus, without a need to demolish the later building, and this temple would be there not only in its ultimate form, as the Romans saw it during the imperial era, but also in its earliest, when it still showed Etruscan forms and was adorned with clay antefixes.[6] Where the Coliseum now stands, we could also admire the vanished Domus Aurea of Nero; on the Piazza del Pantheon we would not only find today's Pantheon,[7] as it was left to us by Hadrian, but also the original building of M. Agrippa in the same spot. Indeed, the same ground would bear the church of Maria sopra Minerva and the old temple over which it is built.[8] And it might only take a change of the direction of our gaze or another perspective on the part of the observer to produce yet another view.

Obviously, there is no point in spinning this fantasy any further since it leads to the unimaginable, even to the absurd. If we want to represent the historical sequence spatially, it can only happen through a juxtaposition in space; the same space cannot be filled in two ways. Our attempt seems to be a pointless indulgence that has only one justification: it demonstrates how far we are from mastering the peculiarities of psychic life through vivid representation.

We should also address one objection. Why have we chosen the past of a

---

6   [Ornamental tiles made of stone or clay.]
7   [Sacred building dedicated to the gods; the largest domed building surviving from ancient times.]
8   [The Church of Santa Maria sopra Minerva in Rome was built over the ruins or foundations of an earlier temple dedicated to the Egyptian goddess Isis, which had been erroneously ascribed to the goddess Minerva.]

city, in particular, in order to compare it with the mental past? The assumption that everything past will be preserved applies to mental life also only on the condition that the organ of the psyche has remained intact and that its tissue has not suffered from trauma or inflammation. Destructive influences that could be equated with such causes of illness, however, are present in the history of any city, even if it had a less turbulent past than Rome and even if, like London, it had hardly ever been ravaged by an enemy. The most peaceful development of a city includes the demolition and replacement of buildings, which is why a city is a priori unsuitable for this kind of comparison with a mental organism.

We yield to this objection and give up the effect of such an impressive contrast by turning to a more closely related object of comparison, such as the animal or human body. But here, too, we find the same thing. The earlier phases of development are no longer preserved in any sense; they have merged into the later phases, for which they provided the material. The embryo cannot be detected in the adult: the thymus gland[9] of the child is replaced by connective tissue after puberty but no longer present itself; in the long bones of an adult human it is possible to trace the contours of the child's bone, but the bone itself disappeared when it stretched and thickened until it assumed its final shape. The fact remains that such a preservation of all preliminary stages, alongside the final formation, is only possible in the mental realm and that we are not capable of properly representing this occurrence.

Perhaps we are going too far with this assumption. Perhaps we should be satisfied with asserting that the past *can* be preserved in mental life and does not *necessarily have to be destroyed*. It is at least possible that in the psychic realm, too, some old things are blurred or consumed—regularly or exceptionally—to such an extent that they can no longer be restored and revived by any process, or that preservation is generally linked to certain favorable conditions. It is possible, but we do not know anything about it. We may only hold on to the fact that the preservation of the past in mental life is the rule rather than the strange exception.

If we are quite ready to acknowledge that an oceanic feeling exists for many people and are inclined to trace it back to an early phase of the sense of self, a further question arises: can this feeling claim to be viewed as the source of religious needs?

---

9   [A lymphoid organ that decreases in size and activity during adolescence.]

I do not consider this claim to be compelling. A feeling can be a source of energy, after all, only if it is itself the expression of a strong need. It seems irrefutable to me that religious needs derive from infantile helplessness and the resulting longing for the father, especially since this feeling does not simply continue on from childhood but is constantly replenished from fear of the overwhelming power of fate. I would not be able to identify a need from childhood that was as strong as that for paternal protection. This displaces from its central place the role of the oceanic feeling, which might aim to restore unrestricted narcissism. One can quite clearly trace the origin of the religious attitude to the child's feeling of helplessness. Other causes may be lurking there, but they remain obscured for now.

I can imagine that the oceanic feeling entered into a relation to religion only at a later point. This sense of oneness with the universe, which is its basic idea, strikes us as a first attempt at religious consolation and like another way of denying the danger that the ego recognizes as threatening from the outside world. I confess, here again, that it is very difficult for me to work with these barely graspable quantities. Another one of my friends, who was driven by an insatiable thirst for knowledge to the most unusual experiments which finally turned him into a know-it-all, assured me that in practicing yoga one can actually awaken new sensations and general feelings in oneself by turning away from the outside world, turning one's attention to bodily functions, and learning special ways of breathing. He regards these general feelings as regressions to ancient, long-sedimented states of our psyche. He sees in them a physiological basis, as it were, of the many wisdoms of mysticism. This would suggest connections to some dark modifications of mental life, such as trance and ecstasy. But I feel the urge to exclaim here in the words of the diver in Schiller's poem:

"For happy is he who breathes in the rosy hues of light."[10]

---

10   [Friedrich Schiller (1759–1805), "The Diver."]

II

n my work *The Future of an Illusion*,[11] I was far less concerned with the deepest sources of religious feeling than with what the common man understands by his religion, about the system of doctrines and promises that on the one hand resolves the riddles of this world with enviable completeness, and on the other, assures him that a diligent providence will watch over his life and make up for any failures in an existence beyond. The common man cannot imagine this providence otherwise than in the figure of a magnificently exalted father. Only such a figure can know the needs of his human offspring, and be mollified by his pleas and appeased by the signs of his repentance. The whole thing is so obviously infantile and detached from reality that it becomes painful for anyone well-disposed toward humanity to realize that the great majority of mortals will never be able to rise above this conception of life. It is even more humiliating to experience how large a number of people alive today—who cannot help but realize that this religion is not tenable—nonetheless try to defend it piece by piece in pitiful skirmishes of retreat. One would like to join the ranks of believers in order to confront the philosophers who believe that the God of religion can be saved by substituting an impersonal, shadowy, abstract principle and admonish them: "Thou shall not take the name of the Lord in vain!" Although some of the greatest minds of the past have done the same, they do not serve as examples. We know why they had to act in this way.

Let us return to the common man and his religion, as the only one which ought to bear this name. First, we encounter the well-known saying of one

---

11 [Freud, *The Future of an Illusion* (1927), where Freud discusses the origins, development and future of religions in the modern world.]

of our great poets and wise men concerning the relationship of religion to art and science:

> Whoever has science and art
> also has religion;
> whoever does not have those two
> should get religion![12]

On the one hand, this saying places religion in opposition to the two highest achievements of human beings; on the other hand, it claims that they can stand for or replace religion in terms of their value for our lives. In our effort to deny religion to the common man, we clearly do not have the poet's authority on our side. We will try a particular approach to fully appreciate this sentence. As life is imposed on us, it is too difficult for us and brings us too much pain and disappointment, and too many impossible tasks. We absolutely need palliatives to endure it. ("We cannot do without provisional constructions of support," the writer Theodor Fontane told us.)[13] There are perhaps three such measures: powerful distractions that make us disregard and attach less importance to our misery; substitute satisfactions that reduce it; and intoxicants that make us insensitive to it. Something of this kind is absolutely required.[14] Voltaire directs our attention toward distractions when he concludes his *Candide* with the advice to cultivate one's garden. Scientific activity is such a distraction as well. The substitute gratifications provided by art are illusions when compared to reality, but they are no less psychologically effective, thanks to the central role played by fantasy in mental life. The intoxicating substances affect our physical body by altering its chemistry. It is not easy to indicate which position religion takes in this series. We will have to take a broader view.

The question of the purpose of human life has been asked innumerable times but has never found a satisfactory answer, and perhaps it does not have one. Some of those who have asked it have added that if it turns out that life has no purpose, then it loses all value for them. But this threat does

---

12 [Johann Wolfgang von] Goethe, "Zahme Xenien," IX (posthumously published poems).

13 [Fontane, German poet and novelist, known for his realism (1819–1898).]

14 In a less elevated idiom, Wilhelm Busch says the same thing in his *Pious Helena* [a widely popular, satirical storybook published in 1872]: "Whoever has worries also has liquor close by."

not change anything. Rather, it seems that one has a right to reject th tion. It seems to rest on that human arrogance of which we already ki	ᴊᴏ many other expressions. There is no talk of a purpose in the life of animals if that purpose, in fact, is not to serve man. But even this idea is not tenable, because humans do not know what to make of many animals—apart from describing, classifying, and studying them—and countless animal species have evaded such use by living and becoming extinct before humans ever laid eyes on them. Once more, it is only religion that knows how to answer the question about the purpose of life. One will hardly go wrong in deciding that the idea of a purpose of life stands and falls with organized religion.

We will therefore turn to the less challenging question of what people themselves reveal through their behavior to be the purpose and intention of their lives. What do they demand from life, and what do they want to achieve in it? It is hard to miss the answer here: they strive for happiness, they want to become happy and stay that way. There are two sides to this striving, a positive and a negative goal. On the one hand, it seeks the absence of pain and discomfort and, on the other, the experience of intense pleasure. In the narrower sense of the word, "happiness" only refers to the latter. According to this dichotomy of goals, human activities unfold in two directions, depending on whether they seek to realize—predominantly or even exclusively—one or the other of these goals.

As we see, it is simply the program of the pleasure principle that defines the purpose of life. This principle governs the performance of the mental apparatus from the beginning; there can be no doubt about its usefulness, and yet its program is at odds with the whole world, with the macrocosm as well as with the microcosm. It is not at all feasible; all the institutions of the universe are opposed to it, and one might say that the intention that man should be "happy" is not contained in the plan of "creation." What is called happiness in the strictest sense arises from the rather sudden satisfaction of highly pent-up needs and, by its nature, is only possible as an episodic phenomenon. When any situation longed for by the pleasure principle is prolonged, it produces only a feeling of lukewarm comfort; we are made in such a way that we can derive intense pleasure only from a contrast and from the continual state itself only very little.[15] In this way our possibilities

---

15   Goethe even warns: "Nothing is more difficult to endure than a series of beautiful days." But this might be an exaggeration. [The original poem reads: "Anything in the world may be endured except a series of beautiful days." Goethe, *Poems,* first published in 1815.]

for happiness are already limited by our constitution. It is far less difficult to experience misfortune. We are threatened with suffering from three directions: from our own body, which, destined to decay and dissolution, cannot even do without pain and fear as warning signals; from the outside world, which can rage against us with overpowering, relentless, destructive forces; and finally from relationships with other people. We may experience the suffering that comes from this last source as more painful than any other. We tend to regard it in some way as a gratuitous ingredient, although it may be a fate no less inevitable for us than the suffering resulting from other causes.

It is no wonder that, under the pressure of these possibilities for suffering, people tend to reduce their demand to be happy, just as the pleasure principle itself transformed under the influence of the outside world into the more modest reality principle. No wonder that we already consider ourselves happy when we have escaped misfortune and survived suffering and that, in general, the task of avoiding suffering relegates that of gaining pleasure to the background. Upon reflection, we can see that one can try to solve this problem in very different ways, all of which have been recommended by the various schools of wisdom and pursued by people throughout time. The unrestricted satisfaction of all needs emerges as the most tempting way of life, but that means putting enjoyment before caution and exacts a punishment after a short while. The other methods, which aim predominantly at the avoidance of discomfort, differ depending on the source of discomfort to which they pay greater attention. There are extreme and moderate procedures, as well as one-sided ones and those that attack several areas at the same time. Intentional isolation and keeping oneself apart from others are the most obvious defense against the suffering that can arise from human relationships. We realize that the happiness that can be achieved on this path is that of lasting quiet. There is no other way to defend yourself against the dreaded outside world than by turning away from it in some way, if you want to solve this task for yourself alone. There is, of course, another and better way. As a member of the human community, we may use technology guided by scientific knowledge to tackle nature and subjugate it to human will. Then you work together with everyone on everyone's happiness. The most intriguing methods for preventing suffering, however, are those that try to influence one's own organism. Finally, all suffering is only a sensation that only exists insofar as we feel it, and we feel it only as a result of the way our organism is set up.

The crudest but also the most effective method of thus exerting influence is chemical intoxication. I do not believe that anyone completely understands how they actually work, but the fact is that there are substances foreign to the body whose presence in our blood and tissue gives us immediate sensations of pleasure but also changes the conditions of our sensory life so that we become unable to receive signals of discomfort. Both effects take place not only simultaneously but also appear to be intricately interconnected. But there must also be substances in our own chemistry with similar effects, because we know at least one pathological state, mania, in which such behavior resembling intoxication occurs without the ingestion of a drug. In addition, our normal mental life fluctuates between easier and more difficult ways of experiencing pleasure, which go hand in hand with a reduced or increased susceptibility to discomfort. It is very regrettable that this toxic dimension of mental processes has so far eluded scientific research. The service provided by intoxicants in the struggle for happiness and in the efforts to keep misery at bay is so highly valued as a benefit that individuals and entire peoples have assigned them a permanent position in their libidinal economy. They are treasured not only for providing immediate sensations of pleasure but also for providing a desperately hoped-for moment of independence from the outside world. We all know that with the help of a liquid or chemical "worry relief" you can escape the pressure of reality at any time and find refuge in a world of your own with better conditions of sensibility. It is well known that precisely this property of intoxicants determines their danger and harmfulness. It is possible that they are to blame for the useless loss of great amounts of energy that could be deployed to improve the human condition.

The complicated structure of our mental apparatus permits quite a few other influences. Just as the satisfaction of an instinct is happiness, it becomes the cause of severe suffering when the outside world deprives us and refuses to satisfy our needs. One can therefore hope to be liberated from a part of suffering by an effort to adjust these instinctual impulses. This kind of defense against suffering no longer attacks the sensory apparatus but instead seeks to gain control over the inner sources of our needs. In an extreme way, this happens by killing off one's urges, as prescribed by life lessons from the Orient and as practiced by yoga. If it succeeds, then one has, of course, also given up all other activities (and sacrificed life itself) and, by another path, acquired once more only the happiness of peaceful quiet. We follow the same path with humbler goals if we strive only for mastery over our instinctual life. In that case, the controlling elements are the higher psychic instances, which have subjected themselves to the reality principle. Here we have by no means abandoned our goal of achieving satisfaction, and we reach a certain protection against suffering in that the non-satisfaction of instincts under control is experienced as less painful than that of uninhibited instincts. The cost, however, is an undeniable reduction in the possibilities of enjoyment. The feeling of happiness derived from the satisfaction of a wild instinctual impulse untamed by the ego is incomparably more intense than that derived from satisfying a domesticated instinct. This may also be an economic explanation for the irresistibility of perverse impulses and for the attraction of the forbidden in general.

Another technique of fending off suffering makes use of the displacement of the libido that our mental apparatus allows and that adds so much flexibility to its functioning. The task here is to displace the instinctual goals in such a way that they cannot be affected by the frustrations of the outside world. This is aided by the sublimation of the instincts. The greatest results can be achieved when one knows how to sufficiently increase the pleasure gained from the sources of mental and intellectual work. Fate can then do little to harm you. The satisfaction of this kind, such as the artist's joy in creating and giving form to his imaginary visions and that of the researcher in solving problems and grasping the truth, has a special quality that we will certainly one day be able to define in metapsychological terms. At the moment we can only say figuratively that they appear to be "more refined and more sophisticated" to us, but their intensity is subdued compared to that derived from the satisfaction of coarse, primary instinctual impulses; they do not convulse our bodily existence. The drawback of this method is that it is not generally applicable and is accessible to but few people. It presupposes special inclinations and talents that only rarely occur at a level where they can be effective. Even to these few talented individuals such gifts cannot afford complete protection against suffering nor create an impenetrable armor against the arrows of fate when one's own body becomes the source of suffering.[16]

---

16   In cases where there is no special inclination that forcefully prescribes a direction to someone's life's interests, a steady profession, accessible to everyone, can take the place indicated by Voltaire's sage advice. It is not possible adequately to appreciate the importance of someone's chosen profession in terms of the libidinal economy in a brief overview. No other technique in the conduct of life

If the just-mentioned procedure already indicates clearly the intention to make oneself independent of the outside world by looking for satisfaction in inner, psychic processes, then the same traits emerge even more strongly in the next one. Here the connection with reality is relaxed even more, and the individual derives satisfaction from illusions recognized as such without letting their deviation from reality diminish his enjoyment. These illusions have their origin in the life of fantasy, which, at the time of the development of one's sense of reality, was expressly withdrawn from the requirements of reality testing and dedicated to the fulfillment of wishes which were difficult to realize. First among these fantasy satisfactions is the pleasure taken in works of art, which the artist's mediation makes available even to those who are not themselves creative.[17] Anyone who is sensitive to the influence of art will not overestimate it as a source of pleasure and consolation in life. But the mild anesthesia that art produces in us in is no more than a fleeting escape from the hardships of life and is not powerful enough to make us forget real misery.

Another, more energetic and thorough procedure identifies reality as the only enemy and as the source of all suffering, with which one cannot live and with which one must sever all relations if one is to be happy in any meaningful sense of that word. The hermit turns his back on this world and doesn't want anything to do with it. But we can do more. We can aim to change the world and construct another one in its place, where the most unbearable features have been erased and replaced by new ones in accordance with our own wishes. Those who pursue this path to happiness in

---

binds the individual so tightly to reality as the emphasis on work, which securely integrates him into at least a part of reality and also into the human community. The possibility of shifting a significant part of one's libidinal components, whether narcissistic, aggressive, and even erotic, to professional work and the interpersonal relationships connected with it, gives one's profession a value no less important than its indispensable role in determining and justifying one's existence in society. A profession is particularly satisfying when it is freely chosen—if it allows a person to make use, by way of sublimating them, of existing tendencies as well as persisting or constitutionally reinforced instinctual impulses. And yet people mostly do not consider a chosen profession as a road to happiness. People do not pursue it like other possibilities of satisfaction. The great majority of people only work because they have to, and this natural reluctance to work results in the most difficult social problems.

17 [See Sigmund Freud, "Formulations on the Two Principles of Mental Functioning" (1911) and *Introductory Lectures on Psychoanalysis*, lecture XXIII (1916–17).]

desperate indignation will usually achieve nothing; reality is too strong for them. Such an individual turns into a madman who usually finds no assistance in enforcing his madness. Some claim, however, that each of us behaves in some way like a paranoid individual when we correct an aspect of the world we cannot tolerate by forming a wish and injecting this imaginary creation into reality. Particularly important, in this regard, are cases in which a large number of people jointly embark on the effort to ensure happiness and ward off suffering by a delusional transformation of reality. The religions of mankind must also be counted as instances of such mass madness. Nobody who still participates in such madness, of course, ever recognizes it as such.

I do not believe that this account of the methods by which people strive to gain happiness and keep away suffering is complete, and I also realize that the material could be arranged differently. I have not yet mentioned another one of these procedures, not because I forgot about it, but because it will concern us in another context. How would it be possible to forget precisely this technique of the art of living! It is distinguished by the most curious combination of specific features. Of course, it also strives for independence from fate (which is the best name for it) and, with this intention, shifts satisfaction to inner mental processes by making use of the above-mentioned displaceability of the libido. But it does not turn away from the outside world and, on the contrary, clings to its objects and gains happiness from an emotional relationship with them. This technique of the art of living is not satisfied with and simply bypasses the rather tired, defeatist goal of avoiding displeasure and instead sticks to the original, passionate striving for positive happiness. Perhaps it really comes closer to that goal than any other method. I mean, of course, that direction of life which takes love as its focus and expects all satisfaction to result from loving and being loved. Such a psychological attitude is close enough for all of us; one of the manifestations of love—sexual love—has given us the strongest experience of an overwhelming sensation of pleasure which provides the model for our pursuit of happiness. What is more natural than to persevere in seeking happiness in the same way that we first encountered it? The weak side of this technique of life is plain to see; otherwise, it would not have occurred to anyone to depart from this path to happiness to seek another one. We are never more unprotected against suffering than when we are in love, never more helplessly unhappy than when we have lost the beloved object or its love. But this account by no means exhausts all dimensions of the technique of life based on the value of love for achieving happiness, and there is much more to say about it.

We may here add the interesting case that happiness in life is predominantly sought out in the enjoyment of beauty, wherever it shows itself to our senses and our judgment: in the beauty of human forms and gestures, natural objects and landscapes, artistic and even scientific creations. This aesthetic approach to realizing our life's goals offers little protection against the threat of suffering, but it can compensate for a lot. The enjoyment of beauty takes the form of a special, mildly intoxicating sensation. The utility of beauty is not clearly evident and its cultural necessity cannot be easily defined, and yet civilization cannot be conceived without it. The branch of philosophy called aesthetics studies the conditions under which the beautiful is experienced, but it has not been able to offer real insight into the nature and origin of beauty. As usual, the lack of results is concealed by a flood of resounding and contentless words. Psychoanalysis, unfortunately, has the least to say about beauty. All that seems certain is that it derives from the area of sexual experience, where beauty would be a perfect example of a goal-inhibited impulse. "Beauty" and "charm" were originally properties of the sexual object. It is remarkable that the genitals themselves, the sight of which is always exciting, are hardly ever judged to be beautiful while, in contrast, the quality of beauty seems to attach to certain secondary sexual characteristics.

In spite of the incompleteness of this account, at this point I venture a few remarks to conclude our investigation. The program which the pleasure principle imposes on us for achieving happiness cannot be fulfilled, but we must not—no, we cannot—give up on our efforts to somehow bring it closer to fulfillment. One may pursue very different paths to get there by emphasizing either the positive content of the goal, namely the increase in pleasure, or the negative one, which is the avoidance of discomfort. In none of these ways can we gain all that we desire. Happiness, in the diminished sense in which we consider it to be something possible, is a problem of the individual's libidinal economy. There is no single piece of advice here that applies to all; everyone must seek his individual path for finding bliss. The greatest variety of factors will prove relevant to direct anyone on their particular path. What matters is how much real satisfaction a person can expect from the outside world, to what extent an individual is prompted to make himself independent of it, and, finally, how strong he imagines himself to be to change it according to his wishes. In addition to external circumstances, the psychological constitution of the individual will be decisive already at this early point. The predominantly erotically inclined individual will put emotional relationships with other people first, while the more self-sufficient narcissistic person will seek essential satisfaction from his inner mental processes, and the man of action will not let go of the outside world against which he can test his strength. For the types of individuals at the midpoint of these tendencies, the nature of their talent and the extent to which they can sublimate their drives will determine where they should shift their interests. Every extreme decision will exact punishment by exposing them to the dangers inherent in the inadequacy of any technique of life chosen at the expense of all others. Just as the careful businessman avoids tying up all his capital in one place, so, too, may life's wisdom counsel us not to expect all satisfaction from a single endeavor. Success is never certain but depends on the confluence of many elements, perhaps none more than the ability of one's psychic constitution to adapt its function to the environment so the latter can be exploited to gain pleasure. Anyone who is endowed with a particularly unfavorable instinctual constitution and has not properly passed through the restructuring and reorganization of his or her libidinal components which is essential for all later achievements will find it difficult to gain happiness from their external situation, especially if they are faced with more challenging tasks. Finally, the life technique that promises such an individual at least some surrogate satisfaction is the escape into a neurotic illness, which one usually performs already at a young age. Anyone who then experiences his or her efforts for happiness to be thwarted in later life can still find consolation in the pleasure gained by chronic intoxication, or they will embark on the desperate attempt of resistance by becoming psychotic.[18]

Religion interferes with this interchange of choice and adaptation by imposing its path toward finding happiness and protection from suffering on everyone in the same way. Its technique consists in lowering the value of life and distorting our image of the real world into a delusion, which presupposes an intimidation of our intelligence. At this price, by forcibly arresting individuals at the stage of psychic infantilism and drawing them

---

18   I feel compelled to point out at least one of the gaps that remain in the above description. A consideration of the human possibilities of happiness should not fail to account for the relative relationship between narcissism and object libido. We have yet to understand what it means for the economy of the libido that it essentially must rely on nothing but itself.

into a mass delusion, religion succeeds in sparing many people from individual neurosis. But hardly anything more; there are, as we have said, many paths that can lead to the happiness which is accessible to man, but none does so reliably. Religion cannot keep its promise either. When the believer finally finds himself compelled to speak of God's "inscrutable counsel," he thereby admits that unconditional submission remains his only option for the final possibility of consolation and source of pleasure in suffering. And if he is prepared for that, he could probably have spared himself the detour.

III

Our investigation of happiness has not taught us much up to this point that is not common knowledge. Even if we proceed with the question of why it is so difficult for people to be happy, the prospect of discovering anything new does not seem much better. We have already given the answer by listing the three sources of our suffering: the superior power of nature; the frailty of our own bodies; the inadequacy of the institutions that regulate the relationships people have with each other in the family, the state, and society. With regard to the first two, we quickly reach a conclusion; we are forced to recognize these sources of suffering and surrender to the inevitable. We will never completely dominate nature; our organism, since it is a part of this nature, will always remain a transitory structure, limited in adaptation and performance. But instead of paralyzing us, this realization points our activities in the right direction. If we cannot remove all suffering, we can at least alleviate some instances and mitigate others, as the experience of many thousands of years has convinced us. We behave differently when it comes to the third source of suffering—that produced by social arrangements. We do not want to accept it at all and cannot understand why the institutions we have created should not provide protection and be a benefit for all of us. But once we consider how badly we have done in preventing this particular type of suffering, we begin to suspect that here, too, some part of nature in its invincibility might be responsible for it, now in the form of our own psychic constitution.

Upon closer examination of this possibility, we encounter such an astonishing assertion that it deserves our sustained attention. It proposes that much of the blame for our suffering stems from our so-called civilization and that we should be much happier if we gave up on it and returned to primitive circumstances. I call it astonishing because—however one may define the term civilization—it is certain that everything we use in order to try to protect ourselves against the threat from various sources of suffering is a product of that same civilization.

How did so many people adopt this stance of a disconcerting hostility towards culture? It seems that a deep and long-standing dissatisfaction with the state of their particular civilization prepared the soil where this condemnation could take root, occasioned by specific historical events. I think I can identify the two most recent of these occasions, but I lack the expertise to trace such events back far enough throughout the history of humanity. This hostility against civilization must already have existed at the historical moment when Christianity defeated the pagan religions. It was certainly closely related to the devaluation of earthly life that is found in Christian doctrine. The second to last event occurred when, during various exploratory expeditions, Westerners came into contact with primitive peoples and tribes. Due to inadequate observation and a flawed understanding of their customs and traditions, such people seemed to the Europeans to lead a simple, happy life with few unmet needs, which remained out of reach for the culturally superior visitors. Based on subsequent encounters, many judgments of this kind were corrected; in many cases, a certain relief in people's daily lives had been wrongly attributed to the absence of complex cultural demands, while its actual causes were the abundance of natural resources and the relative ease in satisfying major needs. We are particularly familiar with the cause of fewer cultural demands; we gained more insight into it when we began to understand the mechanism of the neuroses which threaten to undermine civilized man's already limited share of happiness. It was discovered that a person becomes neurotic because he cannot tolerate the amount of renunciation that society imposes on him in the service of its cultural ideals, and it was concluded that when these requirements are removed or greatly reduced, he could return to other opportunities for happiness.

There is yet another factor to cause disappointment. Over the past few generations, human beings have made extraordinary advances in the natural sciences and their technical application and consolidated man's dominion over nature in previously unimaginable ways. The details of these advances are so well known that they need not be listed here. People take pride in these achievements, and rightly so. But they have begun to notice that this newly gained control over space and time, this subjugation of the forces of nature and the fulfillment of thousand-year-old longings did not satisfy their craving for pleasure or make them palpably happier. This statement should lead us to conclude merely that power over nature is not the only condition for human happiness, just as it is not the only goal of the endeavors of culture, but not to deduce from it the general worthlessness of technical advances for the achievement of our happiness. One might object: Is it not a net gain in pleasure and an unequivocal increase in happiness if I can hear as often as I want the voice of my child who lives hundreds of miles away from me, and if I can learn in the shortest time after a friend has arrived somewhere that he safely completed the long, arduous journey? Is it not significant that medicine has succeeded in so extraordinarily reducing the mortality of small children and the risk of infection in childbearing women and indeed in extending the average lifespan of individuals in civilized nations by a considerable number of years? There are a great number of additional benefits of this kind, which we owe to the much-maligned age of scientific and technical progress. But at this point, we hear the pessimism of critical voices that warn that most of these satisfactions followed the pattern of that "cheap pleasure" touted in a particular anecdote. You obtain such pleasure by sticking a naked leg out from under the blanket on a cold winter night and then pulling it back in. If there were no railroad to cover great distances, the child would never have left your hometown and you wouldn't need a telephone to hear his voice. If trans-oceanic travel had not been instituted, my friend would not have ventured across the sea and I wouldn't need to wait for a telegraph to relieve my worries about him. Of what use is the reduction in child mortality if it forces us to exercise the utmost restraint in procreation so that, on the whole, we do not raise more children than in the period before the rule of hygiene, and sexual life in marriage has become more difficult, probably now working against benevolent, natural selection? And finally, what is the point of a long life for us when it is arduous, poor in joyful pleasures, and so painful that we can welcome death only as a redeemer?

It seems certain that we are not comfortable in the civilization of today, but it is very difficult to properly grasp whether and to what extent people in earlier times felt happier and what role their cultural conditions played in this. We will always have the tendency to define misery objectively, which means projecting ourselves into these conditions according to our expectations and sensitivities in order to examine what would make people happy or unhappy there. This kind of observation, which appears objective because it disregards the variation in subjective sensibility, is, of course, the most subjective possible since it substitutes one's own mental state for all other, unknown mental states. But happiness is something quite subjective. No matter how much we recoil from certain situations, that of the ancient galley slave, the peasant in the Thirty Years' War, the victim of the Holy Inquisition, the Jew awaiting the pogrom, it is still impossible for us to empathize with these people and discover in what ways a person's susceptibility to experiences of pleasure and displeasure has been transformed by the original numbness, gradual desensitization, cessation of expectations, and coarser and finer modes of narcotization. If extreme suffering is within the range of possibility, certain mental defense mechanisms are also activated. It seems pointless to me to further pursue this side of the problem.

It is time we directed our attention to the essence of this civilization, whose value for happiness has been put into doubt. We will not demand a concise formulation of this essence before learning something from further examination. Suffice it to repeat[19] that the word "civilization" denotes all of the achievements and institutions that mark the distance of our lives from that of our animal ancestors and that serve two purposes: the protection of humans against nature and the regulation of the relationships between humans. To understand this better, we shall examine the disparate features of civilization as they become apparent in human communities. In doing so, we can readily take as our guide the use of everyday language, or, as it is also called, our feeling for language, with the confidence that this approach will do justice to internal perceptions that still resist expression in abstract terms.

The first step is easy. We recognize as cultural all activities and values that are useful to man by making earth serviceable to him, protecting him against the violence of the forces of nature, etc. There are few doubts about this aspect of culture. If we go back far enough, we realize that the first cultural acts were the use of tools, the taming of fire, the construction of inhabitable shelters. Among them, the taming of fire stands out as a quite extraordinary, unprecedented achievement,[20] while with the others human

---

19   [See Freud, *The Future of an Illusion* (1927).]

20   The material produced by psychoanalysis, while incomplete and not reliably interpretable, allows at least one—fantastic-sounding—conjecture about the origin of this tremendous human feat. It is as though primitive man had been used to satisfying an infantile lust whenever he encountered a fire by extinguishing it with his urine stream. According to existing legends, there can be no doubt about the original phallic conception of the licking flame rising upward. Extinguishing a fire

beings embarked on paths that they have pursued further ever since, the motivation for which is easy to guess. With all of their tools, humans perfect their motor skills as well as sensory organs or remove barriers to their deployment. Engines provide them with enormous powers that they can send, like muscular strength, in any direction taken by ships and planes so that neither water nor air can hinder their movement. With glasses, they correct the defects of their eyesight; with the telescope, they look into remote distances; with the microscope, they overcome the limits of visibility defined by the structure of the retina. With the photographic camera, they have created an instrument that captures fleeting visual impressions, while the gramophone record achieves the same for equally ephemeral sound impressions. Both inventions are essentially material versions of the faculty of recollection and memory, that is given to them. With the help of the telephone, they can hear from distances that even fairy tales would regard as unreachable. Originally, writing is the language of what is absent, and the home a substitute for the womb, which remains the first, probably still longed-for dwelling, in which one had been safe and felt so comfortable.

Everything the human being has produced through science and technology on this earth, where he first appeared as a weak kind of animal in which every individual of his species, in turn, first arrives—"oh inch of nature!"[21]—as a helpless infant, does not only sound like a fairy tale but is the direct fulfillment of all—or most—fairy tale wishes. He can define all of these possessions as achievements of civilization. For a long time already, he had created an ideal conception of omnipotence and omniscience in the image of his gods. He attributed everything to them that seemed

---

by urinating on it—as the later giant children Gulliver in Lilliput [in Jonathan Swift's satirical 1726 *Gulliver's Travels*] and [François] Rabelais's Gargantua [in *Gargantua*, 1534] still resort to—was akin to a sexual act with a man, a pleasure of male potency in a homosexual competition. Whoever was first to renounce this pleasure and spared the fire and could then carry it away with him and force it into his service. By dampening the fire of his own sexual arousal, he had tamed the natural force of fire. This great conquest of civilization would thus be the reward for a renunciation of one's instincts. And further, it is as if the woman had been appointed to keep the fire imprisoned in the domestic hearth because her anatomical structure prohibits her from giving in to such an attempt at pleasure. It is also noteworthy how regularly the experiences during analysis testify to the connection between ambition, fire, and the eroticism of urine.

21 [Cited in the original English; the quote is usually attributed to *Pericles*, a play assumed by scholars in Freud's time to have been partly written by William Shakespeare.]

unattainable to his wishes or was forbidden to him. In this sense, these gods can be said to be ideals of civilization. Now man has come very close to achieving this ideal and has almost become a god himself, if only in the way that ideals are usually achieved according to general human judgment. Not completely; in some areas, not at all, in others, only just halfway. Man has become, so to speak, a kind of prosthetic god who is quite formidable when he puts on all his auxiliary organs, but they have not yet fused into a natural part of him and occasionally still give him a lot of trouble. Incidentally, he can rightly draw some consolation from the fact that this development will not quite conclude with the year 1930 AD. Future times will lead to new, probably unimaginably great advances in this area of civilization, which will further increase man's likeness to God. For the purposes of our investigation, however, we do not want to forget that today's man does not feel happy in his likeness to God.

We recognize, then, that a country has achieved a high degree of civilization if we find that everything that can assist in the exploitation of the earth's resources by man and in his protection against the forces of nature—everything, in short, that is of use to him—is well-organized and effectively carried out. In such a country, flood-prone rivers are regulated in their course, and their water is directed via canals to places where it is lacking. The soil is carefully worked and planted with suitable plants, while the mineral treasures in its depths are diligently mined and processed into needed tools and machinery. The means of transportation are plentiful, quick, and reliable, wild and dangerous animals have been exterminated, and domesticated animals are raised to great success. But we place additional demands on culture that we hope, remarkably, to find realized in the same countries. As if we wanted to deny our first claim of utility, we also welcome it as a sign of civilization when people turn their care and attention to things that are not at all useful and seem rather useless, e.g., if the green spaces necessary in a town to be used as playgrounds and air reservoirs also have flower beds, or if the windows of peoples' homes are decorated with flower pots. We soon notice that this useless part, which we expect civilization to value, is beauty. We require civilized man to revere beauty wherever he encounters it in nature and to manufacture it for objects to the extent he is capable of doing so. But we demand far more from civilization than this. We further ask to see signs of cleanliness and order. We do not think highly of the civilization of an English country town during Shakespeare's time when we read that a tall dung heap was found outside the door of his father's house in Stratford; we are indignant and criticize it as "barbaric," which is the opposite of cultured, when we find the paths of the Vienna Woods strewn with discarded papers.[22] Uncleanliness of any kind seems to us to be incompatible with civilization, and we extend this requirement of cleanliness to the human body as well. We hear with astonishment what a foul smell the person of the *Roi Soleil* [Sun King] used to exude and shake our heads when we are shown the tiny basin on Isola Bella that Napoleon used for his morning toilet.[23] We are not even surprised if someone directly identifies the use of soap as a measure of civilization. It is similar with order, which, like cleanliness, is entirely linked to human effort. But while we must not expect cleanliness in nature, order has rather been imitated from nature. The observation of the great regularities of astronomy provided man not only with the model but also with the first clues for how to introduce order into his life. Order is a kind of repetition compulsion that, once instituted, decides when, where, and how something should be done so that in every similar case there is no need to hesitate and waver. The benefit of order is undeniable because it enables people to make the best use of space and time while protecting their psychic powers. It seems justified for us to expect that order would easily prevail in human activities from the outset, and we are right to be astonished that this is not the case but that instead, people show a natural tendency to be careless, irregular, and unreliable in their work and must first be tediously trained to imitate the celestial models.

Beauty, cleanliness, and order obviously occupy a special place among the requirements of civilization. Nobody would claim that they are as vitally important as control over the forces of nature and other factors we have yet to consider, but nobody would want to dismiss them as minor issues. That civilization is concerned not only with utility is already shown by the example of beauty, which we must include among the interests of civilization. The usefulness of order is completely evident, and when it comes to cleanliness, we have to consider that it is also required by hygiene, and we can assume that this connection was not entirely unfamiliar to people even before disease prevention became a matter of science. But usefulness does

---

22   [Stratford-upon-Avon, birthplace of William Shakespeare. The "Vienna Woods" are a large public park in Vienna, Austria, where Freud lived at the time.]
23   [The Sun King was the name given to King Louis XIV, the ruler of France from 1643 to 1715; Napoleon and his wife Joséphine de Beauharnais visited Isola Bella, an island in Italy's Lago Maggiore, in 1800.]

not fully explain why people strive for these achievements; something else must play a role here.

No other trait seems to characterize civilization better than the esteem and cultivation of higher mental activities—man's intellectual, scientific, and artistic achievements—and the leading role given to ideas in human life. Foremost among these ideas are the religious systems, on whose intricate structure I have tried to shed light elsewhere.[24] Next we find philosophical speculation and, finally, what can be called human ideals, which are our conceptions of the possible perfection of the individual, of the people, and of humanity as a whole, as well as the demands we make on the basis of such ideas. The fact that these creations are not independent of one another but rather intimately interwoven makes both their presentation and their psychological derivation more difficult. If we assume quite generally that the mainspring of all human activities is the striving for the two converging goals of utility and the attainment of pleasure, then the same must apply to the cultural expressions cited here, although this seems readily apparent only for scientific and artistic activity. But there can be no doubt that the other activities also correspond to strong needs, if perhaps to those only found among a minority. Nor should we become distracted by our value judgments about some of these religious and philosophical systems and these ideals; whether we consider them to be the highest achievement of the human spirit or whether we deplore them as aberrations, we must recognize that their presence, and especially their predominance, signifies a high level of civilization.

As the last and certainly not the least important defining trait of a civilization, we need to recognize the way in which people's social relationships with each other are regulated, which concern other people as neighbors, helpmates, sexual objects, or members of a family or state. Here it is especially difficult to steer clear of certain ideal conceptions and to define clearly what is civilized in general. We may begin by declaring that an instance of civilization occurs already with the first attempt at regulating these social relationships. If such an attempt were not made, these relationships would be subject to the will of the individual, which means that the physically stronger individual would decide them according to his interests and instinctual impulses. This pattern would not change if the stronger individual encountered an even stronger one. Human coexistence only becomes

---

24   [See Freud, *The Future of an Illusion* (1927).]

possible when a majority comes together that is stronger than any separate individual and bonds together against all separate individuals. The power of this community now appears as "lawful right" in opposition to the power of the individual, which is condemned as "brute force." This replacement of the power of the individual with that of the community constitutes the decisive step of civilization. The essence of it consists in the fact that the members of the community restrict their possibilities for achieving satisfaction, while the individual knew no such limit. The next requirement of civilization, therefore, is that of justice, which is the assurance that the existing legal order will not be shattered again in favor of an individual. This does not determine the ethical value of such a legal order. In its further development, civilization seems to move towards ensuring that this right is no longer the expression of the will of a small community, such as a caste, social class, or ethnic group, which yet again behaves like a violent individual toward other and perhaps even more numerous collectives. The end result should be a rule of law to which all—at least those capable of entering into a community—have contributed with the sacrifice of their instinctual impulses and which does not let anyone—again with the same exception—become the victim of brute force.

Individual freedom is not an achievement of civilization. It was greatest prior to any civilization, but then mostly without value because the individual was hardly able to defend it. The development of civilization imposes restrictions on individual freedom, and justice demands that no one be spared these restrictions. What stirs in a human community as the urge for freedom can be a form of rebellion against an existing injustice, which could contribute to the further development of civilization and remain compatible with it. But it can also emanate from the remains of the original personality that has not been restrained by civilization and thus become the basis of general hostility to civilization. The urge for freedom is directed against certain forms and claims of civilization—or against civilization in general. It does not seem that any kind of influence will compel man to transform his nature into that of a termite; he will probably always defend his claim to individual freedom against the will of the masses. A good part of the struggle of humanity culminates in the task of finding an expedient balance—one that will bring happiness—between the demands of the individual and those of the masses under civilization. It is one of humanity's fateful problems whether this balance can be achieved through a particular form of civilization or whether the conflict is irreconcilable.

By letting common sense tell us which traits in people's lives are to be called civilized, we have obtained a clear impression of the general picture of civilization, even if initially we did not learn anything not commonly known. In doing so, we have been careful to avoid agreeing with the prejudice that civilization is synonymous with perfection and that it constitutes the path to perfection that is preordained for human beings. But now we are compelled by an idea that may lead in a different direction. The development of civilization appears to us as a peculiar process that happens to humanity and seems familiar in some aspects. We can characterize this process by the changes it causes in the familiar human instincts, the satisfaction of which is the economic task of our lives. Some of these instincts are consumed in such a way that something appears in their place that we describe as an individual's characteristic trait. We found the most remarkable example of this process in the anal eroticism of young human beings. Their original interest in the excretory function, its organs and products is transformed over the course of growing up into a group of traits known to us as frugality, sense of order, and, cleanliness. Though in and of themselves valuable and welcome, they can grow ever more conspicuous and finally dominate and then result in what is called the anal character. We do not know how this happens, but there is no doubt that this view is correct.[25] We have also discovered that order and cleanliness are essential demands of civilization, although their necessity for life is not exactly obvious, any more than is their suitability as sources of pleasure. At this point, we could not fail to note the similarity between the process of civilization and the development of an individual's libido. Other instincts are prompted to displace and redirect onto other paths the conditions for their satisfaction, which in most cases coincides with *sublimation* (of the instinctual aims), with which we are already familiar, while in other cases these processes still remain separate. The sublimation of instincts is a particularly prominent feature in the development of civilization; it allows higher, namely scientific, artistic, and ideological psychic activities to play such a significant part in civilized life. If we yield to a first impression, we are tempted to say that sublimation is the general fate of the instincts, forced upon them by culture. But here further reflection is advisable. Finally, and this seems most important, it is impossible to overlook the extent to which civilization is built upon the

---

25 Freud, "Character and Anal Eroticism" (1908) and numerous other contributions by Ernest Jones and others.

renunciation of instincts and how much it presupposes the non-satisfaction (suppression, repression or something else?) of powerful instincts. This "cultural renunciation" dominates the vast domain of interpersonal relations; as we already know, it is the source of the hostility with which all civilizations have to contend. It also places heavy demands on our scientific work, and there is a great deal to explain here. It is not easy to understand how it is possible to deprive an instinct of its satisfaction. To do so involves considerable risk, and if one does not compensate for it economically, one can expect serious disturbances.

But if we want to know the value of our conception of the development of civilization as a specific process comparable to the normal maturation of the individual, we have to address another problem. We have to answer the question as to what influences the development of civilization owes its origin, how it came into being, and what determined its course.

IV

This task seems so overwhelming that one may admit to being daunted by it. Here are the few points I have been able to discern.

After primitive man had discovered that—quite literally—he had it in his own hands to improve his lot on earth through work, he could not be indifferent to whether another person worked with or against him. This other person acquired for him the value of a co-worker with whom it was useful to live alongside. Even before that, in his ape-like past, he had adopted the habit of forming families; the members of the family were probably his first helpers. Presumably, the founding of the family was connected with the fact that the need for genital satisfaction no longer appeared like a guest who suddenly showed up and, for a long time after departing, was not heard from again but now settled down as a permanent tenant with the individual. This gave the male a motive to keep the female or, more generally, his sexual objects near him, while the females did not want to be separated from their helpless young and now, also in their interest, had to stay with the stronger male.[26]

---

26 The organic, periodic recurrence of the sexual process has been preserved, but its influence on psychic sexual arousal has turned rather into its opposite. This change is most likely related to the receding of the olfactory stimuli through which the menstrual process acted on the male psyche. Their role was taken over by facial stimuli, which, in contrast to the intermittent olfactory stimuli, could maintain a permanent effect. The taboo around menstruation stems from this "organic repression" as a defense against a phase of development that has been overcome; all other motivations are likely to be of a secondary nature (cf. C. D. Daly, "Hindu Mythology and the Castration Complex," *Imago* XIII, 1927). This process is repeated on a different level when the gods of an outdated period of civilization turn into demons. The receding of the olfactory stimuli seems in itself to be the result of man's turning away from the ground and the decision to walk upright, which now makes

In this primitive family an essential feature of civilization is still lacking; the arbitrary power of the father, as the head of the family, was unlimited. In *Totem and Taboo*, I tried to show the path that led from this family to the next level of coexistence in the form of brotherhoods. In overpowering the father, the sons had learned through experience that a union can be stronger than a single individual. Totemic culture is based on the restrictions that they had to impose on one another in order to maintain the new state of living together. The rules governing their taboos were the first "rule of law." The coexistence of human beings was therefore based on two factors: the compulsion to work, prompted by external needs, and the power of love, which prompted the male not to relinquish the sexual object of the female

---

the previously covered genitals visible and in need of protection, and thus creates a sense of shame. The beginning of the fateful process of civilization seems to be the moment when the human assumes an upright posture. From here, the chain runs from the devaluation of the olfactory stimuli and the isolation of women during their menstrual period to the preponderance of facial stimuli, the genitals becoming visible, the continuity of sexual arousal, and finally the founding of the family and thus to the threshold of human civilization. This is only a theoretical speculation, but significant enough to deserve exact research into the living conditions of those animals that are close to humans.

There is also an unmistakable social factor at work in the cultural striving for cleanliness, which finds subsequent justification in hygienic considerations that had already found expression before this insight. The motivation for cleanliness arises from the urge to get rid of the excrement that has become unpleasant to the senses. We know that it is different in the children's nursery. The excrement arouses no disgust in the child and seems valuable to him as a detached part of his body. Education here pushes with particular vehemence towards accelerating the impending course of development, which is intended to make the excrement worthless, disgusting, abominable, and reprehensible. Such a revaluation would scarcely be possible if these substances, withdrawn from the body, were not condemned by their strong odors to share in the fate reserved for olfactory stimuli after man stood upright from the ground. Anal eroticism thus initially succumbs to the "organic repression" that paved the way to civilization. The social factor responsible for the further transformation of anal eroticism is attested to by the fact that, despite all the advances in development, the smell of one's own excrement is hardly offensive to man, but only that of the excretions of others. The unclean individual, i.e., the one who does not conceal his excrement, insults the other and shows no consideration for him, which also finds its expression in the strongest, most common insults. It would also be incomprehensible that humans should use the name of their most faithful friend in the animal kingdom as a swear word if the dog did not attract man's contempt for two of his traits: that dogs are scent-oriented animals that do not shy away from excrement and that dogs are not ashamed of their sexual functions.

and the female not to relinquish the child—a part which has been separated from her. Eros and Ananke have also become the parents of human civilization. The first success of civilization was that a larger number of people could now remain in a community. And since both of these great forces contributed jointly to this, one might expect that all further development would unfold smoothly, towards an ever improved control of the outside world and an ever greater number of people who belong to a community. It is not easy to understand how this civilization could have any other than exhilarating effects on its participants.

Before examining how this process can be disrupted, we allow ourselves to be distracted by recognizing love as a foundation of civilization, which also fills a void in an earlier discussion. We said that the experience of sexual (genital) love grants human beings the strongest experiences of satisfaction and actually gives them the model for all happiness. This ought to suggest to the individual that happiness in life should continue to be sought in the area of sexual relationships, which would place genital eroticism at the center of life. We further established that in doing so he makes himself dependent in a most precarious way on a part of the outside world, namely his chosen love object, and exposes himself to the greatest suffering if he is spurned by it or if he loses it due to infidelity or death. For this reason, the wise men of every age have strongly advised against this way of life, and yet it has not lost its appeal for a great number of people.

A small minority are able, thanks to their constitution, to find happiness via the path of love, although for this to occur there have to be extensive, mental changes in the function of love. These individuals make themselves independent of the consent of the beloved object by displacing the main value of being loved to their own activity of loving. They protect themselves against losing the object by directing their love not at individual objects but equally at all people, and they avoid the fluctuations and disappointments of genital love by redirecting it from its sexual aim and transforming this drive into a *goal-inhibited* impulse. The state of a consistent, undeviating, tender feeling that they achieve in this way no longer bears much external resemblance to the wildly agitated, genital love life from which it had been derived. St. Francis of Assisi may have achieved more than most in thus exploiting love for an inner feeling of happiness. What we can identify as one of the techniques for satisfying the pleasure principle has also been achieved in many ways by religion, with which it may be connected in those remote regions where the distinction between the ego and external objects and the objects among themselves is neglected. From an ethical perspective, the deeper motivation of which will yet become clear to us, this readiness for a general love of all humanity and of the entire world seems to be the loftiest disposition to which any human may ascend. But already at this point we want to register our two main objections to this view. A love that does not choose seems to lose some of its own value by doing an injustice to the object. Furthermore, not all people are lovable.

The love that founded the family remains effective in civilization in both its original form, in which it does not renounce direct sexual satisfaction, and also in modified form as goal-inhibited tenderness. In both forms, it continues its function of binding together a greater number of people in a more intensive way than that achieved by shared professional interests. The careless use of the word "love" in language has a genetic justification. Love is the name for the relationship between man and woman who have founded a family due to their genital needs, but love is also the name for the positive feelings between parents and children, and between siblings in the family, although we have to characterize this relationship as goal-inhibited love, which is tenderness. Goal-inhibited love had originally been fully sensual love—and it remains that in our unconscious. Both fully sensual and goal-inhibited love extend beyond the family and create new bonds with people who had been strangers. Genital love leads to the formation of new families and goal-inhibited love to "friendships," which become important for civilization because they evade some restrictions of genital love, for instance, its exclusivity. But over the course of the development of civilization, the relationship between love and civilization becomes more ambiguous. On the one hand, love resists the interests of civilization, while on the other hand, civilization threatens love with painful restrictions.

This split seems inevitable; the reason for it is not immediately apparent. It manifests itself first as a conflict between the family and the larger community to which the individual belongs. We have already guessed that one of the main strivings of civilization is to cluster people into large units. But the family does not want to release the individual. The closer the family members are, the more they are often inclined to isolate themselves from others, and the more difficult it is for them to enter the larger sphere of life. The phylogenetically older way of closely living together, which existed only in childhood, struggles against being replaced by the form later acquired through civilization. Detachment from the family becomes a task for every adolescent, and society often supports him in resolving it through puberty and initiation rites. It can easily seem that these difficulties are inherent in all psychical, and, in fact, all every organic development.

Furthermore, women soon come into opposition to the course of civilization and begin to delay and restrain it—the same individuals who originally had laid the foundation of civilization through the demands of their love. Women represent the interests of the family and of sexual life while the work of civilization has increasingly become a matter for men, which confronts them with ever more difficult tasks and forces them to sublimate their instincts in ways for which women are not well matched. Since a human being does not have unlimited quantities of psychic energy at his disposal, he has to accomplish his tasks by appropriately distributing his libido. What he consumes for the purposes of civilization, he withdraws largely from women and sexual life. Spending a lot of time with only men on whose relationships he depends alienates him even from his duties as husband and father. Thus the woman finds herself forced into the background by the demands of civilization and enters into a hostile relationship with it.

On the part of civilization, the tendency to restrict sexual life is no less apparent than the other tendency—toward expanding the sphere of civilization. Even the first phase of culture, which is totemic, includes the prohibition against an incestuous choice of objects, perhaps the most drastic mutilation that human love life has experienced over the course of time. Taboos, laws, and customs create further restrictions that affect both men and women. Not all civilizations go equally far in this way; the economic structure of society also affects how much sexual freedom remains. Here, as we already know, civilization follows the requirements of economic necessity since it has to withdraw from sexuality a large amount of the psychic energy which it itself consumes. In this respect, civilization treats sexuality the way a tribe or a segment of the population treats another group it has subjugated in order to exploit it. Fear of the uprising of the oppressed results in tougher precautionary measures. Our Western European civilization marks a high point in this development. It is psychologically completely justified for it to begin with disdain for the expressions of the child's sexual life because there is no chance of curtailing the adult's sexual desires if this had not been prepared in childhood. But there is no justification whatsoever for the fact that civilized society has gone so far as to deny the very existence of these easily demonstrable, even striking phenomena. The choice of an object for the sexually mature individual is restricted to the opposite sex, and most extra-genital gratifications are forbidden as perversions. These prohibitions amount to a demand for a sexual life that takes the same form for all, which ignores the variations in the innate and acquired sexual constitution of human beings, deprives quite a number of them of sexual enjoyment, and thus becomes the source of grave injustice. These restrictive measures could now result in a situation that for those who are normal and not constitutionally prevented from doing so, all sexual interests flow undiminished into the available and open channels. But even heterosexual, genital love, which remains free from ostracism, is further impaired by the restrictions of its legitimacy and of monogamy. Today's civilization makes it very clear that it wants to allow sexual relationships only on the basis of a unique, indissoluble bond between a man and a woman, and that it does not like sexuality as an independent source of pleasure and will only tolerate it as a thus far irreplaceable source for the continuation of humanity.

This, of course, is an extreme position. It is known that it has proven impossible to implement, even for shorter periods. Only the weak have submitted to such a far-reaching intrusion into their sexual freedom, and stronger natures only on a condition that compensates them for it, which will be discussed later. Civilized society has felt compelled to tacitly allow many transgressions, which, according to its statutes, it ought to have prosecuted. But we must not make the opposite mistake and assume that such a cultural attitude is, in fact, harmless because it does not achieve all of its intentions. The sexual life of civilized man is seriously damaged; it sometimes gives the impression of a function in decline, the way our teeth and the hair on our heads seem to decline as organs. It is probably correct to assume that its importance as a source of feelings of happiness, and therefore in the fulfillment of our purpose in life, has diminished considerably.[27] Sometimes it seems to us that it is not just the pressure of culture, but something in the nature of the function itself that refuses to give us full satisfaction and pushes us toward other paths. This may be an erroneous assumption; it is difficult to decide.[28]

---

27 Among the literary writings of the sensitive and well-known English author John Galsworthy [1867–1933], I value in particular an early short story entitled "The Apple Tree." It compellingly shows that the life of today's civilized man leaves no room for the simple and natural love of two human beings.

28 The following remarks are meant to support the observations expressed above: The human being is a kind of animal (like others) with an unequivocally

bisexual disposition. The individual corresponds to a fusion of two symmetrical halves, of which some researchers believe that one is purely male and the other female. It is equally possible that each half was originally hermaphroditic. Sexuality is a biological fact that, though of extraordinary importance to our mental life, is difficult to grasp psychologically. We are used to saying: every human being shows both male and female instinctual impulses, needs, and properties, but the character of male and female can be determined by the study of anatomy yet not by psychology. For psychology, the difference of the sexes fades into an opposition of activity and passivity, whereby we all too thoughtlessly equate activity with masculinity and passivity with femininity, which is by no means confirmed without exception in the animal kingdom. The doctrine of bisexuality is still very much in the dark, and the fact that it has not yet been linked with the doctrine of the drives causes a serious disturbance in the field of psychoanalysis. Whatever the case may be, if we indeed assume that the individual wants to satisfy both male and female desires in his sexual life, we are prepared for the possibility that these demands will not be satisfied by the same object and that they will interfere with each other if it is not possible to keep them apart and direct each impulse onto its special and appropriate path. Another difficulty results from the fact that erotic relationships, in addition to their own sadistic component, are so often accompanied by a certain amount of direct aggression. The love object will not always show as much understanding and tolerance towards these complications as the peasant woman who complains that her husband no longer loves her since he had not beaten her for a week.

The most far-reaching assumption, however, which is based on the explanations in note 25, is that when man started walking upright and devalued the sense of smell, all of sexuality, and not just anal eroticism, threatened to fall victim to organic repression. Since that point, then, the sexual function has been accompanied by a reluctance that cannot be further justified and which prevents full satisfaction and reorients us away from the sexual goal towards sublimations and displacements of our libido. I am aware that Bleuler (1913) has pointed out the existence of such a primary repelling attitude towards sexual life. The fact that *"inter urinas et faeces nascimur"* [we are born between urine and feces] offends all neurotics and many others beside them. The genitals also produce strong olfactory sensations, which many people cannot bear and which turn sexual intercourse into something unpleasant. The deepest root of the sexual repression which advances along with the rise in civilization would be the organic defense of the new form of life resulting from man's upright gait against his earlier animal existence. This scientific discovery has a peculiar parallel in banal and often loudly expressed prejudices. Thus far, these are only unproven possibilities that have not been substantiated by science. We also do not want to forget that despite the undeniable devaluation of olfactory stimuli there exist entire groups of people, even in Europe, who value strong genital odors, which are so unpleasant for us, as sexual stimulants that they will not do without. (See the collections of folklore obtained via Ivan Bloch's surveys: "On the olfactory sense in the *vita sexualis*," in several volumes of *Anthroprophyteia*, edited by Friedrich S. Krauss.)

V

Psychoanalytic work has taught us that precisely these frustrations of sexual life are not tolerated by so-called neurotics. They create substitute gratifications for themselves through their symptoms, but these either create suffering in themselves or become a source of suffering by causing difficulties with society and the world around them. The latter effect is easy to understand, while the former predicament presents us with a new riddle. But civilization demands additional sacrifices besides that of sexual satisfaction.

We interpreted the difficulties in the development of civilization as a general developmental difficulty by tracing them back to the inertia of the libido and its reluctance to abandon an old position for a new one. We say roughly the same when we derive the opposition between civilization and sexuality from the fact that sexual love is a relationship between two people in which a third party can only be superfluous or disturbing, while civilization is based on relationships among a larger number of people. At the height of a love affair, there remains no interest in the environment; the two lovers are sufficient for themselves and do not even need their child in order to be happy. In no other case does Eros reveal the core of its being so clearly and its intention to make one out of several, but when it has achieved this, as has become proverbial, in the love of two people for each other, it does not want to go beyond that.

So far, we can quite well imagine that a cultural community would consist of such doubled individuals who, libidinally satisfied in themselves, are linked to one another by the bond of a professional or shared-interest group. In such a case, civilization would not need to withdraw energy from sexuality. But this desirable state does not and never has existed; reality shows us that culture is not satisfied with the ties that it has so far been able to claim. It also wants to bind the members of the community to one another in a libidinal way and, by using all available means, supports any path that establishes strong identifications among them and enlists the greatest possible amount of goal-inhibited libido to strengthen the bonds of community through friendship. In order to accomplish these goals, the restriction of sexual life becomes inevitable. Yet we have no insight into the necessity that forces culture on this path and justifies its opposition to sexuality. There must exist a disturbing factor that we have not yet discovered.

A clue may be offered by one of the ideal demands, as they are called, of civilized society. It says: "Thou shalt love thy neighbor as thyself." It is world-famous and certainly older than Christianity, which presents it as its proudest claim, but surely not very ancient; in historical times it was still alien to people. Let us approach it naively, as if hearing it for the first time. Then we cannot suppress a feeling of surprise and alienation. Why should we do this? How is it supposed to help us? But most of all, how do we do it? How is it possible for us? My love is something precious to me that I must not renounce without justification. It imposes duties on me that I must be ready to fulfill with sacrifices. If I love someone else, he must in some way deserve it. (I disregard the use he can provide for me, as well as his possible value as a sexual object for me; these two types of relationship are no options for the rule to love one's neighbor.) He deserves this love when he is similar to me in such important ways that I can love myself in him; he deserves it when he is so much more perfect than I that I can love my ideal of myself in him; I have to love him if he is my friend's son because the friend's pain, if he were to suffer, would also be my pain which I would have to share. But if he is a stranger to me and cannot attract me by any value of his own or any already existing significance that he would add to my emotional life, it becomes difficult for me to love him. In fact, I am committing an injustice because my love is valued by all those who belong to me as evidence that I prefer them; it is an injustice to them if I put a stranger on equal footing with them. But if I am expected to love him with that worldly love, just because he is also a being on this planet, like an insect, an earthworm, and a grass snake, then I fear that he will receive a small amount of love, and never as much as I am reasonably justified to retain for myself. What is the point of such a solemnly proclaimed rule if its fulfillment cannot be recommended as sensible?

On closer inspection, I discover even more difficulties. This stranger is not only generally unlovable, but I must honestly confess that he has a greater claim to my hostility and even to my hatred. He does not seem to have the slightest love for me and does not show me the slightest consideration. If it benefits him in some way, he has no qualms about harming me, nor does he consider whether the amount of his benefit corresponds to the amount of damage he does to me. Yes, he doesn't even need to benefit from it; if he can only satisfy any sort of desire with it, he thinks nothing of mocking me, insulting me, slandering me, proving his power over me, and the safer he feels and the more helpless I am, the more surely I can expect him to behave in this way against me. If he behaves differently and shows me, as a stranger, consideration and care, I am unconditionally prepared, without requiring this rule, to repay him in a similar way. Yes, if that grand commandment were to read: "Love thy neighbor as thy neighbor loves thee," then I would not object. There is a second commandment that seems even more incomprehensible to me and unleashes even more violent resistance in me. It says: "Love thy enemies." If I really think about it, I am wrong to dismiss it as an even stronger imposition. It is basically the same.[29]

I think I can now perceive this warning coming from a dignified voice: "Precisely because your neighbor is not lovable and more likely to be your enemy, you should love him as you love yourself." I then understand that this is a similar case to that of *Credo quia absurdum* [I believe because it is absurd].

Now it is very likely that when the neighbor is directly asked to love me as he does himself, he will answer in exactly the way I have done and reject me for the same reasons. I hope that he will not have the same objective right to do so, but he will mean the same thing. After all, there are differences in the behavior of people, which ethics classifies as "good" and "bad" by ignoring the conditions that gave rise to it. As long as these undeniable differences are not eliminated, adhering to the high ethical demands means causing damage to the intentions of civilization by setting up direct rewards for being evil. Here we cannot help but remember an event that took place

---

29   A great poet can allow himself—at least in jest—to express strongly disdained psychological truths. Thus Heinrich Heine admits: "Mine is a most peaceable disposition. My wishes are: a humble cottage with a thatched roof, but a good bed, good food, the freshest milk and butter, flowers in front of my window, and a few fine trees in front of my door; and if God wants to make my happiness complete, he will grant me the joy of seeing about six or seven of my enemies hanging from those trees. Before their deaths I shall, moved in my heart, forgive them all the wrong they did me in their lifetime. One must, it is true, forgive one's enemies—but not before they have been hanged" (Heinrich Heine, *Thoughts and Ideas*).

in the French Parliament during a debate about the death penalty; one speaker had campaigned passionately for its abolition and received tumultuous applause until a voice from the hall called out: "*Que messieurs les assassins commencent!*"[30]

The part of reality that is often denied behind all of this is that man is not a gentle creature in need of love, who at most is able to defend himself when attacked, but that the human being can count among his instinctual gifts also a large proportion of the tendency to aggression. As a result, his neighbor is not only a possible helpmate and a sexual object but also the temptation to satisfy the aggression against him, to use his labor without compensation, to use him sexually without his consent, to take possession of his belongings, to humiliate him, to cause him pain, to torture and kill him. *Homo homini lupus* [man is a wolf to man]. Given all of the experiences of life and history, who has the courage to dispute this statement? Usually, man's cruel aggression waits to be provoked or serves another purpose, the goal of which could also be achieved by gentler means. When circumstances are favorable for it and the opposing mental forces that otherwise inhibit it have disappeared, it also expresses itself spontaneously and reveals people to be wild beasts for whom the protection of their own species is alien. Anyone who recalls the atrocities of the Great Migration, of the invasions of the Huns, of the so-called Mongols under Genghis Khan and Timur, of the conquest of Jerusalem by the pious crusaders, and even the horrors of the last World War, will have to humbly accept the truthfulness of this view.[31]

The existence of this tendency to aggression, which we can sense in ourselves and are justified to assume to exist in others, is the element that disturbs our relationship with our neighbor and forces civilization to make its tremendous efforts. As a result of this primary hostility of people against each other, civilized society is constantly threatened with disintegration. The shared interests of a collective of workers would not hold it together; instinctual passions are stronger than reasonable interests. Civilization has to muster everything possible to impose limits on the aggressive drives of

---

30   ["May the honorable murderers make the first move!"]
31   [The Great Migration here refers to the migratory movement of people in Europe from about AD 300 to 800. Genghis Khan (1162–1227) conquered parts of Central Asia and today's China, where he ruled from 1206 to 1227. Timur (1336–1405) was the undefeated Turco-Mongol conqueror Timur the Lame, who tried to recover the Mongolian empire. In 1099, the then Muslim governed city of Jerusalem was conquered by Christian crusaders.]

people and to suppress them from being expressed through the formation of psychical reactions. Hence the array of methods that are supposed to drive people to identification and goal-inhibited love relationships, hence the restriction of sexual life and therefore also the ideal command to love one's neighbor as oneself, which is actually justified by the fact that nothing else runs so contrary to original human nature. With all its efforts, this endeavor of civilization has not achieved very much so far. It hopes to prevent the roughest excesses of brute violence by granting itself the right to exercise violence on criminals, but the law is unable to grasp the more tentative and subtler expressions of human aggression. The time comes when each of us has to abandon as illusions the expectations attached to our fellow human beings in our youth, and each of us will experience how difficult and painful our lives are made by their ill will. But it would be wrong to reproach civilization as if it wanted to exclude contests and competition from human activities. These are certainly indispensable, but opposition is not necessarily hostility yet is merely misused as an occasion for enmity.

The communists believe to have discovered the way to deliver us from evil. Man is unequivocally good and well-disposed towards his neighbor, but the establishment of private property has corrupted his nature. Ownership of private goods gives power to an individual and with it the temptation to mistreat one's neighbor; the one excluded from possession must rebel in hostility against the oppressor. If private property is abolished, all goods become collectively owned, and all people are allowed to enjoy them, ill will and hostility among people will disappear. Since all needs are satisfied, nobody will have any reason to see the other as his enemy; all will willingly carry out the necessary work. The economic criticism of the communist system is not my concern, and I cannot examine whether the abolition of private property is expedient and beneficial.[32] But I am able to recognize its psychological presupposition as an untenable illusion. With the abolition of private property, one deprives the human appetite for aggression of one

---

32   Whoever has tasted the misery of poverty in his youth and experienced the indifference and arrogance of those who own property should be well insulated against any suspicion that he lacks understanding and goodwill toward efforts to combat the inequality of wealth among people and all of its consequences. Of course, if this struggle is based on the abstract demand for justice derived from the equality of all people, an objection immediately comes to mind—that nature has created injustices through the extremely uneven distribution of physical endowment and intellectual talent among individuals, for which there is no remedy.

of its powerful tools, though certainly not the most powerful. This changes nothing in the differences in power and influence which aggression abuses for its purposes, and also nothing in its essence. Aggression was not created by property but had prevailed almost unrestrictedly in prehistoric times when property was still very paltry. It is already evident in the nursery, when property has scarcely given up its original anal form, and it is the foundation for all tender love relationships among people, perhaps with the sole exception of a mother and her male child. If one removes the personal right to material goods, the privilege arising from sexual relations still remains, which then becomes the source of the strongest envy and the most violent hostility among people who are otherwise on an equal footing. If this privilege is also abolished through the complete liberation of sexual life, namely by eliminating the family and with it the nucleus of culture, there is truly no way to predict which new paths the development of civilization can take. One thing, however, can be expected: that the indestructible trait of aggression in human nature will follow along this way, too.

It is clearly not easy for people to give up on the satisfaction of their aggressive tendencies; they are not comfortable with it. The advantage of a smaller sphere of civilization, which provides the instinct with a release by treating all outsiders as hostile strangers, is not to be underestimated. It is always possible to bind a greater number of people together in love, if only some others remain against whom aggression can be expressed. I once discussed the phenomenon that neighboring and also otherwise close communities feud and mock one another, such as Spaniards and Portuguese, Northern and Southern Germans, English and Scots, etc. I called this the "narcissism of small differences," which does not offer much of an explanation. We can recognize this phenomenon as a comfortable and relatively harmless way of satisfying the tendency to aggression, which makes it easier for the members of the community to stick together. The people of the Jews, scattered everywhere, have in this way rendered respectable services for the civilizations of their host peoples; unfortunately, all the massacres of Jews in the Middle Ages were not enough to make that age more peaceful and safer for its Christian comrades. After the apostle Paul had made universal human love the foundation of his Christian community, the extreme intolerance of Christianity towards those who remained outside became an inevitable consequence.[33] For the Romans, who had not based their

---

33   [Paul the Apostle, also called Saint Paul (5–64/67 AD), was a Christian apostle

community of the state on love, religious intolerance was an alien concept, although with them religion was a matter of the state and the state was imbued with religion. It was also no incomprehensible coincidence that the dream of Germanic world domination called for anti-Semitism to supplement it, and it can be understood how the attempt to establish a new communist culture in Russia finds its psychological support in the persecution of the bourgeoisie. One worries only what the Soviets will do after having exterminated their bourgeoisie.

If civilization imposes such great sacrifices not only on sexuality but also on man's tendency to aggression, we can now understand better that it is difficult for man to find himself happy in it. In fact, primitive man had an easier time in this regard, as he did not experience any restrictions on his instincts. As a counterbalance, he had very little certainty that he would enjoy such happiness for long. Civilized man has traded in a piece of happiness for a piece of security. But we do not want to forget that in the primitive family only the head of the family enjoyed such freedom for his instincts; the others lived in slavish oppression. In that prehistoric period of civilization, the contrast between a minority enjoying the advantages of civilization and a majority deprived of these advantages was thus pushed to its extreme. Through more careful research we have learned from primitive people who exist today that such an individual's instinctual life is by no means to be envied for its freedom. It is subject to restrictions of a different kind but perhaps of greater severity than those of modern civilized man.

If we justly object to our present state of civilization for how inadequately it fulfills our demands for a happy way of life and how much suffering it allows, which could probably be avoided if we tried to uncover the roots of its imperfection with ruthless honesty, we are certainly entitled to do so without showing ourselves to be enemies of civilization. We can expect to gradually implement the kinds of changes in our civilization that enable it to better satisfy our needs and escape such criticism. But we may also come to realize that there are difficulties inherent in the very nature of civilization that will not give way to any attempt at reform. In addition to the tasks of restricting our instincts, for which we are prepared, we are faced with the danger of a condition that can be called "the psychological misery of the masses." This danger is most urgent where the social bond is created

---

(though not one of the original twelve apostles) who spread the teachings of Christianity during the first century; his writings form part of the New Testament.]

mainly through the identification of the participants with one another and where individuals with leadership qualities do not acquire the importance they should in the formation of the masses.[34] The current state of American culture would provide a good opportunity for studying this damage to civilization which is to be feared. But I will avoid the temptation to embark on a critique of American culture; I do not want to give the impression that I am trying to use American methods myself.

---

34   See Freud, *Group Psychology and the Analysis of the Ego* (1921).

VI

I n none of my other writings have I had such a strong feeling as here that I am describing things that are generally known and that I am using up paper, ink, typesetting work, and printing materials in order to talk about matters that are actually self-evident. I am therefore happy to address the fact that the recognition of a particular, independent instinct for aggression seems to constitute a real modification of the psychoanalytic theory of the instincts.

It will turn out that this is not the case and that it is simply a question of more clearly defining a change in our conception that has been accomplished long ago and of following up on its consequences. Of all the slowly developed parts of psychoanalytic theory, the theory of the instincts was put forward with the greatest difficulty. And yet it was so indispensable to the theory as a whole that something had to be put in its place. In the complete perplexity that characterized the initial phases of my theorizing, a sentence by the poet-philosopher Schiller provided the first clue that "hunger and love" hold together the workings of the world.[35] Hunger could be regarded as representing those instincts that want to preserve the individual, while love strives for objects; their main function, favored in every way by nature, is the preservation of the species. Initially, then, ego instincts and object instincts appeared in opposition to one another. For the energy of the latter, and for it exclusively, I introduced the name libido. This marks the full extent of the opposition between the ego instincts and the object-oriented "libidinal" instincts of love. One of these object instincts, the sadistic one, was unique in that its goal was not at all loving and that in some ways

---

35   [Friedrich Schiller (German author; 1759–1805), from his poem "The World's Sages": "Meanwhile, until the world is held / together by philosophy / it maintains itself / with hunger and with love."]

it appeared conjoined with the ego instincts. This instinct also could not hide its close relationship with instincts of mastery which have no libidinal intent. But it was possible to make sense of this inconsistency; quite evidently sadism is part of sexual life, and cruel play could replace tender play. The neurosis appeared as the outcome of a struggle between the interests of self-preservation and the demands of the libido. It is a struggle in which the ego had triumphed, but at the cost of severe suffering and renunciation.

Any analyst will admit that even today this does not sound like an error long since overcome. But one assumption had to be modified as our research progressed from the repressed to the repressive—from the object drives to the ego. The decisive factor here was the introduction of the term narcissism, that is, the insight that the libido attaches itself also to the ego, which is even its original home and, to a certain extent, remains its headquarters. This narcissistic libido turns towards the objects and in this way becomes object-libido and can be transformed back into narcissistic libido. The term narcissism made it possible to gain an analytic understanding of the traumatic neurosis, as well as of many affections bordering on the psychoses and of psychoses themselves. There was no need to abandon the interpretation of the transference neuroses as attempts by the ego to defend itself against sexuality, but this put the concept of libido in jeopardy. Since the ego instincts were also libidinal, it seemed for a while inevitable to make the libido coincide with instinctual energy in general, as C. G. Jung had advocated earlier. But something remained in the way of an as yet unprovable certainty that the instincts cannot all be of the same kind. I took the next step in *Beyond the Pleasure Principle* (1920) when I first noticed the compulsion to repeat and the conservative character of instinctual life. On the basis of speculations about the beginning of life and of parallels in biology, I drew the conclusion that, besides the drive to preserve living matter and to combine it into ever larger units, there must be another, opposing drive, which seeks to dissolve these units and convert them into a primordial, inorganic state.[36] Thus, besides Eros, there had to be a death drive; the interaction and mutual opposition of these two could explain the phenomena of life. Now it was not easy to uncover the workings of this assumed death drive. The utterances of Eros were noticeable and noisy enough; one could

---

36 The opposition which thus emerges between the incessant tendency of Eros toward extension and the generally conservative nature of the instincts is conspicuous and may become a starting point for formulating further problems to investigate.

assume that the death drive labored silently inside the living being to cause its dissolution, but of course that was no proof. A more promising idea was that a part of the drive turns against the outside world and then emerges as the drive to aggression and destruction. The drive itself would thus be forced into the service of Eros so that instead of itself, the organism would destroy other animate and inanimate things. Conversely, the restriction of outer-directed aggression would lead to an increase in self-destruction, which always takes place anyway. At the same time, one could guess from this example that the two types of instincts rarely—perhaps never—appear in isolation from one another but are rather alloyed with each other into different, constantly varying mixtures, which makes them unrecognizable to our judgment. In sadism, long recognized as a partial instinct of sexuality, we encounter a particularly strong amalgamation of the strivings of love with the destructive drive, as in its counterpart, masochism, we find a combination of inwardly directed destruction with sexuality, which makes the otherwise imperceptible destructive trend conspicuous and tangible.

The assumption of the existence of an instinct of death or destruction drive has met with resistance even in psychoanalytic circles; I know that there is often a tendency to ascribe everything that is found dangerous and hostile in love to an original bipolarity which is inherent to it. At first I had only tentatively put forward the views developed here, but in the course of time they have gained such power over me that I can no longer think otherwise. I consider them to be far more useful theoretically than any other possible views since they simplify matters without neglecting or violating the facts, which is the aim of scientific work. I recognize that sadism and masochism have always presented to us the erotically tinged expressions of the outer- and inner-directed destructive drive, but I no longer understand how we could overlook and miss the ubiquity of non-erotic aggression and destruction and fail to give it its due position in the interpretation of life. (The desire for destruction which is directed toward the inside mostly eludes our perception, of course, unless it has an erotic tinge.) I recall my own defensiveness when the idea of the destructive instinct first appeared in psychoanalytic literature and how long it took for me to become receptive to it. I am less surprised that others showed, and still show, the same attitude of rejection. For the little children do not like to hear any mention of man's innate tendency for "evil," for aggression, destruction, and thus also for cruelty. God created them in the image of his own perfection, after all, and we do not want to be reminded of how difficult it is—despite the assurances of Christian Science—to reconcile the undeniable existence of evil with his omnipotence and ever-lasting goodness. The existence of the devil would provide the best excuse for God, and he would play the same role of providing relief in the overall economy of the world which is performed by the Jew in the world of the Aryan ideal. But even then: one is equally justified in asking God to account for the existence of the devil as for that of the evil which he embodies. In the face of these difficulties, each of us will be well advised to take a deep bow at the right moments before man's deeply moral nature. This will make us generally quite popular and earn us forgiveness for quite a few things.[37]

The term "libido" can once more be used to refer to the forceful manifestations of Eros in order to distinguish them from the energy of the death drive.[38] It must be admitted that it is so much more difficult for us to grasp the death drive, which we discern only as something like a residue behind Eros and which remains completely hidden wherever its presence is not betrayed through its amalgamation with Eros. In sadism, where the death drive redirects the erotic aim for its purpose while fully satisfying the sexual urge, we gain the clearest insight into its nature and its relationship to Eros. But even where it appears without any sexual intent and even in the most blind destructive rage, we cannot fail to recognize that its satisfaction is

---

37 In Goethe's figure of Mephistopheles, the identification of the evil principle with the destructive instinct is particularly convincing:

> And justly so: for all things, from the Void
> Called forth, deserve to be destroyed:
> ['Twere better, then, were naught created.]
> Thus, all which you as Sin have rated,—
> Destruction,—aught with Evil blent,—
> That is my proper element.

The devil himself names as his adversary not the sacred and the good, but the power of nature to procreate and increase life—that is Eros.

> From Water, Earth, and Air unfolding,
> A thousand germs break forth and grow,
> In dry, and wet, and warm, and chilly;
> And had I not the Flame reserved, why, really,
> There's nothing special of my own to show.

[Goethe, *Faust* I, part I, scene 3. Translation by Bayard Taylor.]

38 Our current point of view may be expressed approximately in the statement that libido plays a part in every instinctual manifestation but that not every part of such manifestation is made up of libido.

tied to an extraordinarily high degree of narcissistic enjoyment because it presents the ego with the fulfilment of its familiar desire for omnipotence. Moderated, tamed, and as it were goal-inhibited, the instinct of destruction—when directed at external objects—must provide the ego with the satisfaction of its vital needs and with control over nature. Since it is assumed to exist basically on theoretical grounds, we must admit that it is not even entirely proof against theoretical objections. But this is how things appear to us now, given the present state of our knowledge; future research and reflection will certainly bring the clarity that will decide the matter.

In what follows, I take the point of view that the tendency to aggression is an original, independent instinctual disposition of man, and I return to the assertion that in it, culture encounters its greatest obstacle. At one point in the course of this investigation, I arrived at the conclusion that civilization is a special process that mankind undergoes, and I am still under the spell of this idea. I may now add that it is a process in the service of Eros, which aims to unite isolated human individuals, and after that families, then tribes, peoples, and finally nations into the great unity of humanity. Why this has to happen, we do not know; this, precisely, would be the doing of Eros. These multitudes of human beings are supposed to be bound to one another in a libidinal way; necessity alone, and the advantages of being part of a collective, will not hold them together. But the natural instinct for aggression in all human beings, the hostility of one against all and all against one, opposes this program of civilization. This aggressive instinct is the derivative and main representative of the death drive, which we have found next to Eros, sharing in its world domination. And now, I think, the meaning of the development of civilization is no longer obscure to us. It must show us the struggle between Eros and death, between the instinct for life and the instinct for destruction, as it takes place in the human species. This struggle is the essential content of life in general, which is why the development of civilization can simply be described as the struggle for the life of the species.[39] And this battle of the giants our nurse-maids want to conclude peacefully with a lullaby about the gentleness of heaven![40]

---

39   We can probably add more concretely: a struggle for life that took its shape after a certain event occurred that is yet to be discovered.
40   ["Eiapopeai vom Himmel" (hushabye from heaven), in Heinrich Heine's satirical poem "Germany: A Winter's Tale" (1844).]

VII

Why do our relatives, the animals, not exhibit such a struggle over civilization? We do not know. Very probably some of them, the bees, ants, and termites, struggled for thousands of years until they arrived at those institutions—insect colonies—that distribute various functions and limit the role of individuals and for which we admire them today. It is indicative of our present condition that we sense that we would not consider ourselves happy in any of these colonies formed by animals or in any of the roles assigned to the individual there. In other animal species, a temporary balance may have been achieved between environmental factors and their internally warring instincts, which then brought their development to a standstill. In primitive man, a new flare-up of the libido may have sparked renewed resistance in the instinct for destruction. There are a great many questions to which as yet there is no answer.

Another question concerns us more directly. What means are used by civilization to inhibit the aggression that opposes it, to render it harmless, or perhaps to eliminate it? Although we have already encountered some of these methods, we apparently have not yet discovered the most important one. We can gain some insights into it by considering the development of the individual. What happens to him that renders his aggression harmless? Something very strange, indeed, that we would not have guessed and that is yet so readily apparent. His aggressiveness is introjected, internalized, but, in fact, it is sent back to where it came from, that is, turned against the self. There it is taken over by a part of the ego that opposes the rest of the ego in the form of a super-ego and now, in the form of our "conscience," exhibits the same strict readiness for aggression against the ego that the ego would have liked to satisfy against other, strange individuals. We call the tension between the severe super-ego and the ego that has been subjugated by it the sense of guilt; it expresses itself as a need for punishment. Civilization thus gains control over the individual's dangerous lust for aggression by weakening, disarming, and then monitoring the impulse via an agency set up inside, like an occupying force stationed in a conquered city.

Psychoanalysts differ from other psychologists in how they conceive of the origin of the sense of guilt, but they, too, struggle to properly account for it. First, if we ask how a person acquires a sense of guilt, we receive an answer that cannot be disputed: we feel guilty (the devout would say "sinful") if we have done something that we recognize as "bad" or "evil." But we quickly notice how little this answer tells us. Perhaps, after some hesitation, we add that even those who have not actually committed any evil deed but merely recognize their intention to do so may consider themselves guilty, which leads us to the question of why the intention is here considered the same as the act. Both cases, however, presuppose that the evil has already been recognized as reprehensible and must not be carried out. How do we make this decision? We have to reject the idea of an original, that is, natural ability to differentiate between good and evil. Frequently, doing some bad or "evil" is not that which is harmful or dangerous to the ego, but, on the contrary, it is also something desirable and pleasurable. This suggests that some external element determines the actual meaning of good and evil. Since his own feelings did not lead man down this path, he must have a motive for submitting to this external influence. It is easy to identify it in man's helplessness and dependence on others and can best be described as our fear of the loss of love. If he loses the love of another person on whom he is dependent, he also forfeits protection from various dangers and exposes himself above all to the danger that this other, powerful presence proves his superiority by punishing him. Evil is therefore initially that for which one is threatened with the loss of love; because we fear such loss, we must avoid it. That is why it makes little difference whether one has already done something evil or whether one yet wants to do it; in both cases the danger arises only when the authority figure discovers it, and in either case it would behave in the same way.

This state of mind is called "bad conscience," but actually it does not deserve this name because at this level the consciousness of guilt is obviously only the fear of losing love, which is a "social" fear. In the case of young children, it can never be anything else, but also in the case of many adults nothing changes except the fact that the larger human community assumes the place of the father or of both parents. That is why adults regularly allow themselves to carry out the evil that promises them comforts if they can only be sure that the authority figures do not find out about it or cannot harm them; their only fear is that of being found out.[41] Present-day society can generally expect this kind of scenario.

A genuine change occurs only once the instance of authority has been internalized with the establishment of a super-ego. This elevates the phenomena of conscience to a new level; in fact, only at this point should we speak of conscience and a sense of guilt.[42] Now the fear of being discovered and, ultimately, also the difference between doing evil and wanting to do evil disappears, because nothing, not even a mere thought, can hide from the super-ego. But now the situation is no longer serious in any real sense, for we believe that the new authority, the super-ego, has no motive for abusing the ego to which it intimately belongs. But the course of its development, which allows what is past and overcome to live on, finds its expression in the fact that things basically remain as they had been at the beginning. The super-ego torments the sinful ego with the same feelings of fear and lurks for opportunities to have it punished by the outside world.

At this second stage of development, our conscience shows a peculiar quality that was alien to the first stage and that is no longer easy to explain. For it behaves more severely and more distrustfully the more virtuous the person is, so that in the end precisely those individuals who come closest to reaching sainthood blame themselves for the worst sinfulness. This means that virtue forfeits a part of its promised reward, while the docile and renouncing self does not enjoy the trust of its mentor but strives, apparently in vain, to acquire it. It is easy to object here that these difficulties are really artificially constructed. The more severe and vigilant conscience is precisely the characteristic of the moral human being, and if the saints pretend to be sinners, they would not be incorrect in doing so with reference to the

---

41   [Jean-Jacques] Rousseau's famous mandarin here comes to mind! [Freud here refers to a thought experiment attributed to Rousseau in Honoré de Balzac's 1835 novel *Father Goriot*, where two Frenchmen discuss whether causing the death of an aged "mandarin" in China through a mental act, with the result of becoming rich, would cause a moral dilemma (see Freud's 1915 *Reflections on War and Death*). The scene actually occurs in François-René de Chateaubriand's 1802 *The Genius of Christianity* as proof of the indestructible evidence of a moral conscience.]

42   Any well-disposed reader will understand and take into account the fact that this overview draws a sharp distinction between processes that, in reality, occur in fluid transitions and that it is not a question of the existence of a super-ego alone but of its relative strength and range of influence. Everything that has been said so far about conscience and guilt is generally known and almost undisputed.

temptations for instinctual gratification to which they are exposed in a particularly high degree. For as is well known, temptations merely increase if they are consistently denied, while they decline at least temporarily if occasionally satisfied. Another fact of the field of ethics, which is so rich in problems, is that misfortune, that is, external frustration, so greatly increases the power of conscience in the super-ego. As long as a person is doing well, his conscience is also gentle and allows the ego to get away with all sorts of things. But when he has suffered a stroke of bad luck, he starts to reflect, recognizes his sinfulness, heightens the demands of his conscience, and abstains and punishes himself with penance.[43] Entire civilizations have behaved in the same way and are still doing so. But this can be easily explained from the original, infantile level of conscience, which is not abandoned after its introjection into the super-ego but persists alongside and behind it. Fate is seen as a substitute for parental authority; if one is unhappy, it means that one is no longer loved by this highest power, and, thus threatened by this loss of love, one bows anew before the replacement of parental authority in the super-ego, which one had wanted to neglect during one's period of happiness. This becomes particularly clear if, in a strictly religious sense, fate is recognized as nothing but the expression of the divine will. The people of Israel had believed themselves to be God's favorite children, and when the great father caused misfortune after misfortune to rain down on his chosen people, they did not despair over this relationship or doubt God's power and justice but rather produced the prophets, who confronted them with their sinfulness and, out of their consciousness of guilt, created the excessively severe rules of their priestly religion. It is remarkable how differently primitive man behaves! If he suffers a misfortune, he does not blame himself but rather the fetish, which apparently has not done what it is supposed to do, and beats it up instead of punishing himself.

We know, therefore, of two origins of the sense of guilt: one arising from the fear of authority, and the other, which arises later, from the fear of the super-ego. The former forces us to renounce instinctual gratifications while the latter, since we cannot hide the persistence of forbidden desires from the super-ego, also demands our punishment. We have also come to account for

---

43   In a delightful short story, "The First Melon I Ever Stole," Mark Twain addresses this advancement of morality through a mishap. His first melon happens to be unripe. I heard Mark Twain tell this little story himself. After pronouncing its title, he paused and wondered as if himself in doubt: "*Was* it the first?" With that he had said everything. The first melon did not remain the only one.

the severity of the super-ego, that is, the demands of conscience. It simply continues the severity of that external authority whose role it assumes and which it partly replaces. We now see how the renunciation of instincts is related to the sense of guilt. Originally, the renunciation of instincts results from our fear of external authority; we renounce satisfaction in order not to lose that authority's love. Once we have renounced in this way, we are even with this authority, so to speak, and there should be no further need to feel guilty. It is different in the case of fear of the super-ego. Here the renunciation of instincts is not enough, because the wish remains and cannot be concealed from the super-ego. In spite of having successfully renounced our instinct, we nonetheless experience a sense of guilt, which turns into a great economic disadvantage for the creation of the super-ego or, we might say, for the formation of conscience. The renunciation of instincts is now no longer fully liberating; virtuous abstinence is no longer rewarded by the assurance of love, and we have replaced the threat of external unhappiness—the loss of love and punishment on the part of the external authority—with permanent internal unhappiness, with the tension arising from a sense of guilt.

These interrelationships are so complicated and at the same time so important that, at the risk of repeating myself, I would like to tackle them from another angle. The chronological order would then be thus: First, the renunciation of instincts owing to fear of aggression by the external authority (this, of course, is what the fear of the loss of love amounts to since love protects against this aggression of punishment). This is followed by the creation of the internal authority and the renunciation of instincts owing to the fear of it, which is the fear of conscience. In the second case, evil deeds are equated with evil intentions, hence a sense of guilt, and a need for punishment. The aggression of conscience preserves the aggression of authority. So far, things have probably been made clear, but how do we account for the way misfortune lends more strength to conscience (of renunciation imposed from the outside) and for the extraordinary severity of conscience in the best and most dutiful individuals? We have already explained these two peculiar traits of conscience but have probably given the impression that these explanations do not clear up everything and leave something unexplained. Here, at last, an idea comes in that is indeed particular to psychoanalysis and foreign to people's ordinary way of thinking. This idea is of a kind that lets us understand why this matter had to appear so confused and opaque. For it says that in the beginning, our conscience (more correctly: the fear, which later becomes conscience) is indeed the cause of the renunciation of instincts, but later this relationship is reversed. Every renunciation of instincts now becomes a dynamic source of conscience, and each new renunciation increases its severity and intolerance. If only we could align it better with what we already know about the history of the origin of conscience, we would be tempted to make this paradoxical statement: conscience is the result of the renunciation of instincts; or: the renunciation of our instincts (imposed on us from outside) creates our conscience, which then demands the further renunciation of instincts.

The contradiction between this statement and what we have said about the genesis of conscience is actually not so great, and there is a way of further reducing it. To illustrate this point better, we will focus on the aggressive instinct and assume that in these situations, it is always a matter of renouncing aggression. This, of course, is only intended to be a preliminary assumption. The effect of the renunciation of instincts on our conscience then takes place in such a way that every bit of aggression that we fail to satisfy is taken over by the super-ego and there increases its aggression (against the ego). It is not quite correct that the original aggression of conscience is the continuation of the severity of external authority and in that way has nothing to do with renunciation. But we can make this discrepancy disappear if we find a different explanation for this first installment of aggression in the super-ego. The child must have developed a considerable amount of aggressiveness toward the authority that prevents him from having his first but also most significant satisfactions, regardless of what kind of instincts he was forced to renounce. Out of necessity, the child was forced to forego the satisfaction of this vengeful aggression. He finds a way out of this difficult economic situation through known mechanisms, by absorbing this unassailable authority into itself through identification, which now becomes the super-ego that acquires all the aggression that one would have liked to have exercised against this authority as a child. The child's ego has to be content with the depressing role of the humiliated authority of the father. As so often, this is a reversal of the situation. "If I were the father and you were the child, I would treat you badly." The relationship between the super-ego and the ego is the return of real relationships between the ego before it was subdivided and an external object, which have been distorted by the wish. That, too, is typical. The essential difference, however, is that the original severity of the super-ego is not—or not primarily—the degree of severity one has experienced from the external object or one expects of it but rather stems from one's own aggression against that object. If that is the case, one can truly claim that conscience first appeared through the suppression of an aggression and was subsequently strengthened through additional such suppressions.

Which of these two views is correct? The earlier one, which seemed so indisputable to us from the perspective of genetics, or the newer one, which so elegantly completes the theory? Apparently, and also according to evidence produced by direct observation, both are justified; they do not conflict with one another and even converge at one point, for the child's vengeful aggression will also be determined by the degree of punitive aggression that he expects from the father. Experience shows, however, that the severity of the super-ego which develops in a child in no way reflects the severity of the treatment he himself has experienced.[44] The severity of the super-ego seems to be independent of the treatment received; even children with a very gentle upbringing can develop a very severe conscience. But it would also be incorrect to exaggerate this independence; it is not difficult to recognize that the severity of a child's upbringing also strongly influences the formation of the child's super-ego. It turns out that in the formation of the super-ego and the emergence of conscience, constitutional factors and external environmental factors work together, which is by no means strange but the general etiological condition of all such processes.[45]

We may also say that when the child reacts to the first major renunciations of his instincts with excessive aggression and corresponding severity of the super-ego, he follows a phylogenetic model that goes beyond the reaction that would be justified in this situation, because the father figure of primitive times was surely terrifying and could be expected to show the utmost degree of aggression. The differences between the two theories of

---

44   As Melanie Klein [1882–1960; Austrian-British author and psychoanalyst] and other English writers have emphasized correctly.

45   In *Psychoanalysis of the Total Personality* (1927), Fr[anz] Alexander accurately assessed the two main types of pathogenic child-rearing: excessive strictness and excessive indulgence, following Aichhorn's study of neglect [*Wayward Youth*, Vienna, 1925; with an introduction by Freud]. The "excessively gentle and indulgent" father will cause the child to form an excessively strict super-ego, because under the influence of the love he receives, the child has no other outlet for aggression than turning inward. For a neglected individual who was raised without love, the tension between the ego and the super-ego disappears; all of his aggression can be directed outwards. If we disregard constitutional factors, which we can presume exist, we can say that a strict conscience results from the interaction of two vital influences: the renunciation of instincts which unleashes aggression, and the experience of love which directs this aggression inward and transfers it to the super-ego.

the genesis of conscience become even more negligible in the passage from the individual to the phylogenetic history of development. But there is a new, significant difference between these two developmental processes. We cannot go beyond the assumption that humanity's sense of guilt stems from the Oedipus complex and was acquired by the brothers' union when the father was killed. At that time, an act of aggression was not suppressed but carried out; but it was the same aggression whose suppression in the child is supposed to be the source of his sense of guilt. Now, it would not surprise me if a reader exclaimed angrily: "So it doesn't matter at all whether you kill your father or not, you definitely acquire a sense of guilt! This certainly should raise some doubts. Either it is incorrect that guilt stems from suppressed aggression, or the entire tale of the killing of the father is a fiction, and the children of prehistoric humans did not kill their fathers any more often than children do today. Incidentally, if it is not a fiction but plausible history, then one would have a case where what happens is exactly what all the world expects to happen, namely, that one feels guilty because one has truly done something that cannot be justified. And for this case, which incidentally happens every day, psychoanalysis owes us an explanation."

This is true and should be remedied, especially because the explanation is no particular secret. If you feel guilty after and because you have committed a wrongdoing, this feeling should rather be called *remorse*. It only relates to a specific deed and presupposes, of course, that a *conscience*, which is the aptitude for feeling guilty, existed already prior to the deed. This kind of repentance, therefore, can never help us in locating the origin of conscience and the sense of guilt in general. The sequence of these everyday situations is usually that an instinctual need has acquired the strength to achieve satisfaction against the conscience, which is, after all, limited in its strength, and that once the need is thus diminished by having been satisfied, the previous balance of power is restored. Psychoanalysis is therefore correct in excluding from the present discussion the case of a sense of guilt out of remorse, however frequently such cases occur and however great their practical importance.

But if the human sense of guilt goes back to the killing of the primordial father, was this not a case of "repentance," after all, and at that time should not have conscience and guilt existed prior to the deed, based on our assumptions? In this case, where did the repentance come from? Surely, this case must clear up the secret surrounding our sense of guilt and put an end to our embarrassment. And, indeed, it does. This repentance was the result of the original emotional ambivalence towards the father. The sons hated him, but they loved him too. Once their hatred had been satisfied by aggression, love emerged out of their repentance about the deed, established the super-ego through identification with the father, endowed it with the father's power as if to punish them for the aggressive deed committed against him, and created the constraints meant to prevent its recurrence. And since the aggressive tendency towards the father kept recurring in the following generations, the feeling of guilt also persisted and was reinforced anew by every aggression that was suppressed and transferred to the super-ego. Now, I think, we can finally grasp two things perfectly clearly: the part played by love in the creation of conscience and the fateful inevitability of the sense of guilt. It really does not matter whether one killed one's father or abstained from this deed, since one will find oneself guilty in both cases, because the feeling of guilt is the expression of the conflict of ambivalence, and the eternal struggle between Eros and the instinct of destruction or death. This conflict is sparked as soon as people are given the task of living together; as long as this community assumes only the form of the family, it must find expression as the Oedipus complex, establish our conscience, and create the first sense of guilt. When efforts are made to enlarge this community, the same conflict will be continued and strengthened in forms determined by our past and further intensify the sense of guilt. Since civilization obeys an inner erotic impulse, which compels it to bind people to each other in an intimately connected group, it can achieve this goal only by an ever-increasing sense of guilt. What was begun in relation to the father is completed in relation to the crowd. If civilization is the necessary course of development from the family to all of humanity, then—as a result of the inherent conflict of ambivalence and of the eternal strife between love and the pursuit of death—there is inextricably bound to it the increase in the sense of guilt, perhaps to a degree that the individual finds difficult to bear. One is reminded of the moving accusation of the great poet [Goethe] against the "heavenly powers":

"To earth, this weary earth, you bring us
To guilt you let us heedless go,
Then let harsh repentance wring us:
For on earth guilt exacts a price of woe!"[46]

---

46   Goethe, "Harp Player's Song," in *Wilhelm Meister's Apprenticeship* [1796].

We may well sigh with resignation upon realizing that some individuals are endowed with the gift of effortlessly pulling up the deepest insights from the vortex of their own feelings, which the rest of us have to find by charting a path through agonizing uncertainty and restless groping.

VIII

At the end of such a journey, the author must ask his readers' for-giveness for not having been a skillful guide who spared them the passage through tedious stretches and arduous detours. Without a doubt, it could be done better; therefore, I will try belatedly to make up for something.

First of all, I suspect readers have the impression that the discussion of guilt goes far beyond the scope of this essay by taking up too much space and relegating all other content, with which it is not always closely related, to the margins. This may have compromised the structure of the essay, but it is quite in keeping with the intention to present the sense of guilt as the most important problem in the development of civilization and to show that the price we pay for our advance in civilization is a loss of happiness through the heightening of the sense of guilt.[47] What still sounds strange in this sentence, which amounts to the final result of our investigation, can probably be traced back to the very peculiar and as yet not well understood

---

47 "Thus conscience does make cowards of us all" [William Shakespeare, *Hamlet*]. The fact that the education of young people at the present time hides from them the role that sexuality will play in their lives is not the only reproach one must raise against it. Education commits another sin in not preparing young people for the aggression of which they are destined to become the object. In sending young people into life with such incorrect psychological orientation, education acts no differently than if one were to outfit people going on a polar expedition with summer clothes and maps of the Italian lakes. What becomes evident here is a certain misuse of ethical demands. The strictness of those demands would not do much harm if education said: "This is how people ought to be in order to be happy and to make others happy; but one must acknowledge the fact that they are not this way." Instead, the young are made to believe that everyone else fulfills all the demands of ethics and is, in essence, virtuous. This is supposed to justify the demand that every young person also become like that.

relationship between the sense of guilt and our consciousness. In common cases of repentance, which we consider normal, the sense of guilt makes itself quite clearly perceptible to our consciousness; hence we are used to saying "consciousness of guilt" instead of sense of guilt. In the study of the neuroses, to which we owe the most valuable clues for an understanding of normal conditions, we discover some contradictory relationships. In one of these affectations, called obsessive-compulsive disorder, the sense of guilt imposes itself all too loudly on consciousness; it dominates the patients' etiology as well as their daily life by permitting hardly anything else to arise. But in most other cases and types of neurosis, the sense of guilt remains completely unconscious, without thereby in any way lessening its effects. Afflicted individuals do not believe us when we propose to them that they feel "unconsciously guilty"; in order for them to understand us at least halfway, we tell them about an unconscious need for punishment through which the sense of guilt is then expressed. But we should not overestimate this relationship to the appearance of a neurosis; even in the case of obsessive-compulsive disorders, there are types of patients who do not perceive their own sense of guilt or who experience it as a tormenting discontent or a kind of anxiety only when it prevents them from carrying out certain actions. Eventually it will be possible for us to understand these things, but we are not there yet. Perhaps here it is helpful to explain that the sense of guilt is basically nothing but a localized variation of anxiety and that in its later phases it coincides entirely with the *anxious fear of the super-ego.* The same extraordinary variations occur in the relations of anxiety to consciousness. Somehow anxiety is at the root of all symptoms; but at times it noisily claims consciousness all for itself, and at others it hides itself so completely that we are compelled to speak of unconscious anxiety, or—if we want a keep our psychological conscience clean, since fear is really just a sensation—of various possibilities of anxiety. Which is why it is quite conceivable that the sense of guilt produced by civilization is not recognized as such, remains largely unconscious, or manifests itself in the forms of discontent and dissatisfaction that are then traced back to other motivations. Religions, at least, have never failed to recognize the role played by guilt in civilization. They come into existence, after all, with the claim, which I had failed to recognize elsewhere,[48] to redeem mankind from this sense of guilt, which they call sin. From the way in which this redemption is achieved

---

48   I am referring to [Freud] *The Future of an Illusion* (1927).

in Christianity, through the sacrificial death of an individual who thereby takes upon himself a guilt common to all, we concluded something about the nature of the first impetus for acquiring this original guilt, which was also the beginning of civilization.[49]

It will not prove decisive but also may not be superfluous for us to explain the meaning of some terms which we may frequently have used too loosely and interchangeably, such as super-ego, conscience, feeling of guilt, need for punishment, and remorse. All of these terms refer to the same situation but name different aspects of it. We have explored the entity of the super-ego with its several different functions, of which conscience is one, alongside others we ascribe to it, which exists in the form of a censor, to monitor and judge the actions and intentions of the ego. The sense of guilt and the harshness of the super-ego are therefore the same as the severity of our conscience; it is the perception assigned to the ego that lets the ego know it is monitored in such a way, and which takes stock of the tension between the ego's strivings and the demands of the super-ego. The anxiety about this critical authority—the wish to be punished—on which the whole relationship rests, is an instinctual expression of the ego that has become masochistic under the influence of the sadistic super-ego, i.e., that deploys a part of its already available instinct for inner destruction to form an erotic attachment to the super-ego. We should not speak of conscience until the presence of the super-ego can be demonstrated; one must admit that the consciousness of guilt exists prior to the super-ego and therefore also prior to our conscience. This consciousness of guilt is then the immediate expression of our fear of external authority, the recognition of the tension between the ego and that authority, as well as the direct result of the conflict between the need for its love and the urge for instinctual satisfaction, the inhibition of which produces aggressiveness. The superimposition of these two layers of the sense of guilt—fear of external and fear of internal authority—has obstructed some insights into the workings of conscience in several ways. Repentance is a general, comprehensive term for the reaction of the ego in cases when we experience a sense of guilt. It contains the only partly transformed sensory material of the underlying anxiety and is itself a punishment which can include the need for punishment. For these reasons, it too can be older than conscience.

It will do no harm to review once more the contradictions that caused

---

49   [Freud] *Totem and Taboo* (1912).

some confusion during this investigation. At one point, our sense of guilt was supposed to result from aggressions that were *not* acted upon, but at another time, and especially at its historical beginning, it was supposed to result from the killing of the father, as an act of aggression that *was* acted upon. But we found a way out of this difficulty. The establishment of an inner authority, the super-ego, fundamentally changed the situation. Earlier, guilt coincided with repentance; we note that the term repentance here describes only the reaction after an aggression has actually been carried out. Afterwards, as a result of the omniscience of the super-ego, the distinction between intended and executed aggression became far less important; now a sense of guilt could be produced by both an act of violence that had been actually carried out—as everyone knows—and by an act that was merely intended—as psychoanalysis has recognized. Beyond this change in the psychological situation, the conflict of ambivalence between the two original instincts has the same effect. It is tempting to consider this as the solution to the problem of the ever-changing relationship between the sense of guilt and consciousness. The sense of guilt that results from repentance for the evil deed should always be conscious, while the sense of guilt that results from perceiving the evil impulse could remain unconscious. But the answer is not that simple, and obsessional neurosis vigorously contradicts it. The second contradiction was that, according to one view, the aggressive energy that one imagines the super-ego to possess merely extends the punishing energy of external authority and keeps it alive in the mind, while another view proposes that it is rather one's own, not fully discharged aggression that is now directed against the inhibiting authority. The first view seemed to fit in better with the history, and the second with the theory of the sense of guilt. More detailed reflection has almost completely blurred the apparently irreconcilable contrast; the only essential and common fact remains that it is an aggression which has been redirected inward. Clinical observation, in turn, has allowed us to distinguish properly between two sources of aggression ascribed to the super-ego, of which in individual cases one or the other has the stronger effect, but which in general work together.

Here, I believe, is the proper place to propose for serious consideration a view I had previously recommended for provisional adoption. The most recent analytical literature shows a preference for the doctrine that every kind of frustration, every thwarted satisfaction of an instinct, leads or could lead to a heightened sense of guilt.[50] I believe our theoretical model will be greatly helped if we accept this to be true only for *aggressive* instincts, and we will not find much that contradicts this assumption. For how can we explain, on dynamic and economic grounds, that in the place of an unfulfilled *erotic* demand there now arises an increased sense of guilt? It only seems possible in a roundabout way that the prevention of erotic satisfaction evokes a certain tendency to aggression against the person who has interfered with that satisfaction, and that this aggression itself has to be suppressed again. But then it is only aggression that transforms into a feeling of guilt by being suppressed and shifted onto the super-ego. I am convinced that we will have a much simpler and clearer account of many processes if we restrict what psychoanalysis has discovered about the sense of guilt to the aggressive instincts. Examining the clinical material does not yield an unambiguous answer in this area, because, according to our assumption, the two types of instinct hardly ever appear in pure form and isolated from one another; yet considering some extreme cases is likely to point in the direction I expect. I am tempted to make provisional use of this stricter conception by applying it to the process of repression. As we have learned, the symptoms of the neuroses are essentially substitute gratifications for unfulfilled sexual desires. In the course of our analytical work we have discovered, to our surprise, that possibly each neurosis conceals a certain amount of unconscious guilt, which in turn reinforces the symptoms by their use as punishment. Now it makes sense to formulate the following sentence: if an instinctual tendency is subject to repression, its libidinal components are converted into symptoms, and its aggressive components into a sense of guilt. Even if this sentence is correct only as an average approximation, it merits our attention.

Some readers of this essay may also get the impression that they have heard the account of the struggle between Eros and the death drive too often. It was supposed to characterize the process of civilization that humanity undergoes, but it was also used to describe the development of the individual and, in addition, was supposed to reveal the secret of organic life in general. It seems unavoidable for us to examine the relationship between these three processes. The recurrence of the same formula is justified by the consideration that the process of civilization for humanity, just like the

---

50 See, especially, E[rnest] Jones, Susan Isaacs, Melanie Klein, and also, as I understand it, by [Theodor] Reik and [Franz] Alexander.

development of the individual, are both vital processes, which means both of them must play a part in the most general characteristic of life. And yet, pointing out this general feature adds nothing that would let us differentiate between them, as long as it is not delimited by special conditions. We can only be comfortable, therefore, when we assert that the process of civilization is a specific modification of the life process that it undergoes under the influence of a task set by Eros and instigated by Ananke (the exigencies of reality) and that this task is that of unifying separate individuals into a community bound together by libidinal ties. But if we focus on the relationship between the process of civilization of humanity and the developmental or educational process of the single human being, we will decide quite readily that the two processes are of a very similar nature, if not even the same process for different objects. The process of civilization of the human species is, of course, an abstraction of a higher order than the development of the individual and, therefore, more difficult to represent clearly, and we should not become obsessed with the search for analogies. But given the similarity of the goals—one being the integration of a separate individual into a unified mass of humans, and the other the creation of such a mass out of many separate individuals—the similarity of both the means to accomplish them and the resulting phenomena will come as no surprise. There is one distinction between the two processes that is of such extraordinary significance that it should not go unmentioned any longer. In the developmental process of the individual, the program of the pleasure principle, which is to find happiness, remains the main goal, while the integration into or adaptation to a human community appears to be an unavoidable condition that must be fulfilled on the way to achieving this goal of happiness. If it could be done without this condition, it might be better. In other words, the development of the individual seems to be a product of the interaction of two trends: the striving for happiness, which we usually call "selfish," and the striving for belonging with others in the community, which we call "altruistic." Neither of these terms reveals much below the surface. In the development of the individual, as I said, the main emphasis is usually placed on the egotistical striving for happiness, while the other, which we call "cultural," is usually content with the restrictive role. It is different with the process of civilization. Here the goal of creating a unified whole of separate individuals is by far the main concern, and while the goal of happiness still exists, it is pushed to the background. It almost seems that the creation of a great human community would be most successful if there were no need to worry about the happiness of the individual. The developmental process of the individual may therefore have distinctive features that are not found in the process of civilization of humanity. The former process has to coincide with the latter only when its aim is to incorporate the individual into the community.

Just as the planet orbits around a central body in addition to rotating on its own axis, so the individual also takes part in the development of mankind while making his own way through life. But to our dull eyes, the play of forces in the night sky seems frozen in an eternally fixed order; while in the organic process, we can still see how the forces contend with one another and how the conflict yields ever-changing results. Just as the two strivings—for individual happiness and for human connection—must battle each other in every individual, so the two processes of the development of the individual and of civilization must confront each other in a struggle and mutually contest their ground. But this struggle between the individual and society does not derive from the probably irreconcilable antagonism of the primordial instincts, Eros and death. It is a conflict in the economy of the libido, comparable to the dispute over how to apportion the libido to the ego and to objects. It reaches its eventual resolution in the individual, such as we may hope for in the future of civilization, however burdensome it proves for the life of the individual at present.

The analogy between the process of civilization and the individual's course of development can be significantly extended. One may correctly say that the community also develops a super-ego, under whose influence the development of civilization takes place. It may be tempting for someone familiar with different civilizations to examine this equation in detail. I will limit myself to highlighting a few conspicuous points. The super-ego of a cultural epoch has a similar origin to that of the individual; it rests on the impression left by great leaders with distinct personalities, people with overwhelming mental and spiritual powers or those in whom some human striving has found the strongest and purest, and hence often the most one-sided, expression. In many cases, the analogy extends even further, in that such individuals were often enough, though not always, mocked, mistreated, or even cruelly disposed of by others during their lifetime, just as the forefather ascended to the status of divinity only long after he was violently killed. The person of Jesus Christ is the most deeply moving example of this fateful conjunction, if, in fact, that figure does not belong to the myth that conjured him into existence out of the obscure memory of that primal event. Another point of agreement is that the cultural super-ego, just like that of the individual, sets up strict ideal demands, non-compliance with which is punished by "fear of conscience." Yes, here we encounter the peculiar case that in this area the mental processes are more familiar to us and more accessible to consciousness from the side of the masses than they can become in the individual. In the individual, only the aggressions of the super-ego make themselves loudly known when tension arises in the form of reproaches, while the demands themselves often remain unconscious in the background. If we bring them to conscious knowledge, we find that they coincide with the regulations imposed by the prevailing cultural super-ego. At this point, we may say that both processes, the cultural developmental process of the crowd and that of the individual, are inextricably fused. This is why some manifestations and properties of the super-ego can be more easily recognized by its behavior in the cultural community than by its behavior in the separate individual.

The cultural super-ego has developed its ideals and made its demands. Among the latter, those that concern the relationships of men to one another are what we call "ethics." At all times, people have placed the greatest value on ethics, as if one expected this discipline to yield particularly important achievements. Indeed, ethics is concerned with that point that is easily recognizable as the sorest spot in any culture. Ethics is therefore to be understood as an attempt at therapy: an effort to achieve with a directive of the super-ego what was previously not achievable through other cultural activities. We already know that the question here is how the greatest obstacle to civilization, the constitutional propensity of people to be aggressive toward one another, can be removed, and for this very reason we are particularly interested in what is probably the most recent of the cultural super-ego commandments: "Love thy neighbor as thyself." Based on the study and therapy of neuroses we reproach the super-ego of the individual on two counts: in the severity of its commandments and prohibitions, it cares too little for the happiness of the ego, and it does not sufficiently account for the resistances against obeying them, which are the instinctual strength of the id and the difficulties found in our material environment. In the course of therapy, we are therefore quite often forced to fight the super-ego and to attempt to lower its demands. We can raise very similar objections against the ethical demands of the cultural super-ego. It also does not take sufficient account of the facts of the human's mental constitution; it issues a commandment without asking whether it is possible for a person to obey it.

On the contrary, it assumes that the human ego is psychologically capable of any task assigned to it and that the ego can have absolute control over its id. That is an error, and even with so-called normal people, the control of the id cannot be pushed beyond certain limits. To ask for more is to prompt rebellion or neurosis in the individual or to make him unhappy. The commandment "Love thy neighbor as thyself" is the strongest defense against human aggression and an excellent example of the unpsychological approach of the cultural super-ego. The commandment is impossible to fulfill; such a great inflation of love can only reduce its value but not eliminate suffering. Civilization neglects all of this; it only admonishes us that the more difficult it is to obey a rule, the more merit there is in doing so. Yet in today's civilization, whoever obeys such a rule only puts himself at a disadvantage compared to those who transgress it. How immense an obstacle to civilization aggression must be, if the defense against aggression can make you as unhappy as aggression itself! What is called natural ethics has nothing to offer in this situation except the narcissistic satisfaction of considering oneself superior to the others. An ethics based on religion here takes recourse to its promises of a better life beyond. I am inclined to think that for as long as virtue is not rewarded on earth, ethics will preach in vain. I have no doubt, too, that a genuine change in people's relation to property will remedy more here than any ethical commandment; yet the recognition of this fact has been obscured by the socialists with yet another idealistic misunderstanding of human nature and thus made useless for practical purposes.

The type of investigation that seeks to trace in the phenomena of the development of civilization the role played by a super-ego promises even further discoveries. I hasten to reach a conclusion, but one question remains that I find difficult to avoid. If the development of civilization so closely resembles and deploys the same means as that of the individual, should we not be justified in our diagnosis that some cultures—or cultural epochs, and possibly all of humanity—have become "neurotic" under the influence of civilizing tendencies? The analytic dissection of these neuroses could be followed by suggestions for therapy which would be of great practical interest. I could not say that such an attempt to apply psychoanalysis to the cultural community would be nonsensical or doomed to yield no results. But one would need to be very careful not to forget that these are merely analogies, after all, and that with people as with concepts, it is dangerous to tear them out of the sphere where they originated and developed.

Moreover, the diagnosis of communal neuroses runs into a particular difficulty. In the case of the individual neurosis, the nearest point of reference is the contrast between the patient and his surroundings, which are assumed to be "normal." For a mass of individuals that is similarly affected, no such background exists; it would have to be brought in from elsewhere. As for the therapeutic application of such an insight, how could the most accurate analysis of a social neurosis be of help since no one has the authority to impose therapy on the masses? Despite all these difficulties, we can expect that one day someone will venture to offer such a pathological study of cultural communities.

For a variety of reasons, it is far from me to provide an evaluation of human civilization. I have tried to distance myself from the enthusiastic prejudice that our civilization is the most precious thing we can own or acquire and that its path will necessarily lead us to heights of undreamt-of perfection. I can at least listen, without indignation, to the critic who thinks that, when considering the goals of civilization and the means used to reach them, one must reach the conclusion that the whole endeavor is not worth the effort and that it could result only in a condition which the individual must find unbearable. It is easy for me to be impartial here since I know very little about these things, and with any certainty only that the value judgments of people are inevitably guided by their desire for happiness, which means they are attempts to prop up their illusions with arguments. I would certainly understand if someone were to emphasize the inevitable character of human civilization and maintain, for example, that the inclination to restrict sexual life or to enforce the humanitarian ideal at the expense of natural selection were developmental trends that cannot be prevented or redirected, and to which we ought best to succumb as if they were necessities of nature. I am also aware of the objection that often in the course of human history, certain strivings which we once considered insurmountable have been cast aside and replaced by others. I therefore lose the courage to stand as a prophet before my fellow men, and I bow to their reproach that I cannot bring them any consolation because that is what they all demand, the wildest revolutionaries no less passionately than the most well-behaved and pious believers.

The fateful question of the human species seems to me to be whether and to what extent the development of its civilization will succeed in bringing under control the disturbance of communal life caused by the human drive for aggression and self-destruction. Perhaps in this context, the present times deserve special interest. Humans have made such strides in controlling the forces of nature that, with their help, it is easy for them to exterminate each other down to the last man. They know this, and this knowledge accounts for a good deal of their current unrest, their unhappiness, their sense of fear. And now it can be expected that the other of the two "heavenly powers," the eternal Eros, will try to assert itself in the battle with its equally immortal adversary. But who can foresee with what success and what result?[51]

---

51   [Freud added the final sentence in 1931, when the rising threat of fascism was already apparent.]

FREUD: THE PSYCHO-ARCHEOLOGY
OF CIVILIZATIONS
by Carl E. Schorske[1]

I n his last decade of life, Sigmund Freud turned once more to a question
which had troubled him ever since he published his conception of the
psyche in *The Interpretation of Dreams* in 1900: What were the implica-
tions of individual psychodynamics for civilization as a whole? His mature
reflections on that subject he set forth in *Civilization and Its Discontents*
(1930). Its somber conclusions have, of course, become part of our self-un-
derstanding: that the progress of our technical mastery over nature and the
perfection of our ethical self-control are achieved at the cost of instinctual
repression in the "civilized" man—a cost so high as not only to make neurotics of individuals, but of whole civilizations. An excess of civilization
could produce its own undoing at the hands of instinct avenging itself
against the culture that had curbed it too well.

One might expect that, in making a point so historical in its essence,
Freud would have reached out to propose a scheme of civilization's march
toward the organization of nature and the collective development of the
superego. Such was not Freud's way. He approached his problem not
historically but analogically, proceeding from an analysis of the individual psyche, its structure and experience, to the functioning and future of
society. Yet to introduce his reader to the difference between the psyche
and history, he had recourse to an ingenious historical metaphor. "Let us
choose," he says, "the Eternal City" to represent the nature of mental life.
Freud asks the reader to consider Rome as a physical entity, from its earliest

1   Carl E. Schorske, Dayton Stockton Professor of History and Director of
European Cultural Studies at Princeton University, delivered this address on 7
December 1979, at the second in the Massachusetts Historical Society's 1979–1980
series of Evening Meetings on Shapers of Contemporary Thought.

beginnings as a fenced settlement on the Palatine through all its many transformations until the present day. Imagine that all the buildings known to the archeologist and the historian stand simultaneously in the same urban space with their modern survivors or successors: "On the Piazza of the Pantheon," Freud explains, "we should find not only the Pantheon of today as bequeathed to us by Hadrian, but on the same site also Agrippa's original edifice; indeed, the same ground would support Santa Maria sopra Minerva and the old temple over which it was built." Freud wishes us to struggle with this multi-faceted vision of the simultaneity of the non-contemporaneous, the Eternal City that is the totality of its undiminished pasts. (With eyes trained by Picasso and the Cubists, it is easier for us to visualize than for him.) But this, he acknowledges, is not possible either in space or time. "Destructive influences are never lacking in the history of any town," he grants, "even if it has had a less chequered past than Rome, even if, like London, it hardly ever has been pillaged by an enemy." Only in the *mind* can what is past survive, after it has been, at the level of consciousness, displaced or replaced; and there, it is "rather the rule than the exception" for it to do so.[2]

Here Freud lets the metaphor of the city as total history drop, turning our attention to the individual mind, the psyche. In the mind of each of us, it is civilization itself—not the pillaging enemy—that destroys the traces of past experience, burying the personal life of instinct under the weight of its censorious denials and demands. But the psychoanalyst can, like the archeologist, recover what is buried and, by restoring a personal history to consciousness, enable us to come to terms with its traumas and even to build it anew.

Is Freud suggesting that, if we could reconstitute the Eternal City in our minds as he has asked us to picture it, with all its pasts laid bare, we would redeem it? He would make no such claim; he only points to the need to recognize that those "immortal adversaries" that inhabit the depths in each of us, Eros and Thanatos, are active and/or repressed in the collective life too, and that the earthly city must deal with them. The model of the individual psyche helps Freud to diagnose the collective life, but not to formulate a social therapy.

Freud's use of Rome in *Civilization and Its Discontents* is highly abstract

---

2   Sigmund Freud, *Civilization and Its Discontents* [trans. Ulrich Baer (New York: Warbler Press, 2022), 7].

and literary, as an image of an unattainable, condensed *summa* of western historical life. Forty years earlier, when he was *nel mezzo del cammin'* and at work on *The Interpretation of Dreams,* Freud had to conjure with Rome in a quite different way, as a central problem of his self-analysis, what he called his "Rome neurosis."[3] Within his dreams of Rome at that time, he excavated in his psycho-archeological dig an earlier Rome that belonged to the days of his childhood. The *via regia* [royal road] to his discovery of the unconscious life led through the Eternal City. Once he had conquered Rome, Freud returned to it again and again. It was the city most strongly related in Freud's mind with psychoanalysis and the one which resonated most fully with all his contradictory values and desires, compacted like the simultaneous totality of historical Romes that he had suggested to the readers of *Civilization and Its Discontents.*

I

Before there was psychoanalysis, before Freud confronted Rome and exhumed it, he was drawn to two modern civilizations—the English and the French. He saw each through the stereoptic lenses of his time and social class. Like many another Austrian liberal, Freud was a passionate Anglophile from his youth. His family experience confirmed his social prejudice. When the Freud family fortunes sustained reverses in the late 1850s, Sigmund's older half-brothers emigrated to build successful careers in Manchester, while father Jacob removed the rest of his family from Freiberg in Moravia to a life of economic hardship in Vienna. After graduation from Gymnasium in 1875, Freud made his first visit to his relatives in England, a visit which left an indelible impression on him. In 1882, newly engaged but deeply frustrated about his career, England surfaced in his consciousness as a kind of land of hope. In a letter to his fiancée, Martha Bernays, Freud gave passionate voice to a longing to escape from Vienna and the shadow of "that abominable tower of St. Stephen"—symbol of Catholic reaction. "I am aching for independence," he wrote, "so as to follow my own wishes. The thought of England surges up before me, with its sober industriousness, its generous devotion to the public weal, the stubbornness and sensitive feeling for justice of its inhabitants, the running fire of general interest that

---

3   ["Nel mezzo del cammin di nostra vita" (Midway upon the journey of our life) is the first line of Dante Alighieri's *The Divine Comedy* (1320).]

can strike sparks in the newspapers; all the ineffaceable impressions of my journey seven years ago, one that had a decisive influence on my whole life, have been awakened in their full vividness."[4]

The "decisive influence" of his early visit to England, if we are to believe a letter Freud wrote to his closest friend immediately on his return in 1875, embraced both professional and intellectual values. England, as the land of "practical works," inclined him away from pure science toward medical practice. "If I wanted to influence many people rather than a small number of readers and co-scientists, then England would be the right country." At the same time, the young freshman bore witness to the impact of English scientific thought: "The acquaintance which I have made with English scientific books will always keep me, in my studies, on the side of the English for whom I have an extremely favorable prejudice: Tyndall, Huxley, Lyle, Darwin, Thomson, Lockyer and others."[5]

In 1882, in his mood of discouragement, Freud fanned the smoldering embers of Anglophilism that remained from his visit with reading of a wider kind. "I am taking up again," he reported to his Martha, "the history of the island, the works of the men who were my real teachers—all of them English or Scotch; and I am recalling again what is for me the most interesting historical period, the reign of the Puritans and Oliver Cromwell." One might have expected that the future liberator of sexuality would have defined his interest in the Puritans negatively. Not at all, for his eye was seeking civic virtue.

"Must we stay here, Martha?" Freud wrote of Vienna. "If we possibly can, let us seek a home where human worth is more respected. A grave in the Centralfriedhof is the most distressing idea I can imagine."[6] Although he seems often to have entertained the idea of emigrating to England in the 1880s, Freud could not shake off his attachment—his biographer Ernest Jones considers it unconscious—to hated Vienna as the scene of his professional self-realization. It was only Hitler that caused him finally to leave for London, in the end to be buried there rather than in the Centralfriedhof [Vienna's main cemetery].

In his devotion to England as an ideal society, Freud only shared an

---

4   Quoted in Ernest Jones, *The Life and Work of Sigmund Freud*, 3 vols. (New York: Basic Books, 1953–1957), I :178–179.

5   Ronald M. Clark, *Freud: The Man and the Cause—A Biography* (New York: Random House, 1980), 38–40.

6   Jones, *Freud*, 1:179.

attitude widespread in the Austrian liberal bourgeoisie before World War I. Indeed, when the Great War broke, Freud, who would soon give "all my libido…to Austria-Hungary," hesitated in his allegiance. As he wrote to Carl Abraham, "I should be with it (Austria-Hungary) with all my heart, if only I could think England would not be on the wrong side."[7]

Within the larger whole, however, there were different kinds of Anglophilism. Most of Freud's contemporaries among the intellectuals admired England for producing a human type who fused bourgeois practicality with aristocratic grace, business, and high style. The writer Arthur Schnitzler portrayed in a novel an Austrian Jew who, making a new life in England, embodied the typical Englishman as Austrians of the *fin de siècle* saw him: cool and gray-eyed, courteous, and self-possessed. The poet Hugo von Hofmannsthal and his friends in the higher bureaucracy wanted to establish a public school on the English model in Austria to breed such personalities. Theodor Herzl's Jewish state too would cultivate such aristocratic realists *à l'anglais*. Adolf Loos, architect and critic of Austria's visual culture, when he founded a journal called *Das Andere* (*The Other*) "to introduce western culture into Austria," exalted the gentlemanly values of sobriety and practicality reflected in English clothing, interior decor, and use-objects.

Freud's Anglophilism showed none of these aristocratic-aesthetic features. He drew his image of England from an older, more militant mid-century liberalism, hostile to aristocracy and to the Catholicism associated with it in Austria. Parliamentarism was what they prized in English politics; philosophic radicalism was their lodestar in culture. Freud studied philosophy under Franz Brentano, a leading protagonist of English positivism in Austria. Under the editorial guidance of Theodor Gomperz, a classicist who, following George Grote, embraced the Sophists and radical democrats as the finest flowers of Athens, Freud worked on the German edition of the complete works of John Stuart Mill. (He translated "On the Subjection of Women," "Socialism," "The Labor Movement," and "Plato.") Though he does not speak of a debt to Bentham, Freud's early theory of instincts, with its duality of pleasure principle and reality principle, resonates with echoes of Bentham's hedonistic system. From the seventeenth to the nineteenth century, those whom Freud claimed as his "real teachers—all of them English or Scotch," were the protagonists of libidinal repression and the advocates

---

7   Ibid, 2:171.

of postponed gratification—whether as Puritan foes of aristocratic squandering and the Church of Rome or as secularized utilitarian moralists. They were builders, stern and rational, of the liberal ego which, for Freud, made of England the classic land of ethical rectitude, manly self-control, and the rule of law.

Freud named all his children after his teachers or their wives—except one. Oliver, his second son, he named for Cromwell. Thus the great sex theorist paid tribute to the public virtues of private repression and the special achievement of English political culture.

II

It has become a commonplace of Freud scholarship to identify Paris with the impact of Jean-Martin Charcot, the great theorist and clinician of hysteria, on Freud's intellectual development. Justly so. Freud went on a fellowship to the Salpêtrière Hospital for Women in 1885 as a neurologist exploring the organic basis of nervous disorders. Charcot turned him in a new direction, toward the study of hysteria, especially hysterical paralysis, as a disease which behaved "as if there were no anatomy of the brain."[8] He also opened Freud's mind, even if only in informal discourse, to "la chose génitale," the sexual component in the etiology of hysteria. When Freud returned to Vienna to open his own practice, it was as a neurologist still, but one with a special interest in "nervous cases" that others found tiresome: patients who did *not* suffer from organic lesions of the nervous system.[9] Thus returning from Paris with a pronounced predilection for what we would now call neurotics, Freud set out for the first time, boldly if only half aware, on the *via regia* to the unconscious.

Freud's letters to his fiancée during his half-year in Paris make it clear that the city itself, or more accurately, his encounter with it, both prepared and reinforced the impact of Charcot.

England was good order, morality, and liberal rationality, appealing to Freud as a possible refuge from the social inequities and professional frustrations of Austria. Paris was the very opposite: a city of danger, of the

---

8   Ibid., 1:233. For an able discussion of Freud's relation to Paris and Charcot somewhat at variance with mine, see Léon Chertok, "Freud in Paris (1885/86)," *Psyche*, 5:431–448 (1973).
9   Marthe Robert, *The Psychoanalytic Revolution: Sigmund Freud's Life and Achievement*, trans. Kenneth Morgan (New York: Harcourt Brace, 1968), 72.

questionable, of the irrational. Freud accepted, but richly elaborated, Paris as the wanton, the female temptress; he approached it in a spirit of adventure at once thrilling and terrifying.

Until he went to Paris in 1885, there is, as far as I could find, no reference to the city in his writings, either as fact or as symbol. More than a decade later, however, in *The Interpretation of Dreams*, he tells the reader cryptically that "Paris...had for many long years been the goal of my longings; and the blissful feelings with which I first set foot on its pavement seemed to me a guarantee that others of my wishes would be fulfilled as well."[10] What wishes? Freud does not say. In the beautiful letters he wrote to his fiancée and her sister during his Paris *Lehrjahr*, however, the intense and impressionable young Freud seems to have opened himself to the whole world of forbidden *fleurs du mal* that Freud the Anglophile and liberal Jew had until then rejected or avoided: the Roman Catholic Church, the bewitching power of the female, and the power of the masses. As London was the city of the ego, where the whole culture supported one's independence and control, Paris was the city of the id, where instincts erotic and thanatal reigned.

Two months after his arrival in Paris, Freud could still write of it, "I am under the full impact of Paris, and, waxing very poetical, could compare it to a vast overdressed Sphinx who gobbles up every foreigner unable to solve her riddles."[11] Freud chose his image well, for the Sphinx united beauty and the beast, challenging natural law with her composite being and rationality with her fateful riddle that only brilliant, perverse Oedipus could solve.

Mindful of the bitter lifelong disgust and mistrust in which Freud held Catholicism, recalling his yearning to escape from the shadow of "that abominable tower of St. Stephen" to England in 1882, we are stunned to watch his reaction to Notre Dame. "My first impression was a sensation I have never had before: 'This is a church.'...I have never seen anything so movingly serious and somber, quite unadorned and very narrow." What Freud reported of the companion with whom he paid his first visit to Notre Dame must have been true of himself: "There he stood, deeply lost in wonder."[12]

---

10   Sigmund Freud, *The Interpretation of Dreams*, trans. and ed. James Strachey (New York: Avon Books, 1965), 228.

11   Sigmund Freud to Minna Bernays, Paris, 3 Dec. 1885, *The Letters of Sigmund Freud*, ed. Ernst L. Freud; trans. Tania and James Stern (New York: McGraw Hill, 1964), 187.

12   Freud to Martha Bernays, Paris, 19 Nov. 1885, *Letters*, 183.

Freud associated himself not only with the beauty of the cathedral, but with its beastly side as well. He later recalled that the platform of Notre Dame was his "favorite resort" in Paris. "Every free afternoon, I used to clamber about there on the towers of the church between the monsters and the devils." When Freud in a dream of omnipotence identified himself with Hercules, he discovered behind the dream Rabelais' Gargantua, avenging himself on the Parisians by turning a stream of urine on them from the top of Notre Dame.[13]

As for the people of Paris, they simply frightened Freud. They struck him as "uncanny." To be sure, political turbulence marked the months of Freud's stay, a period of governmental instability (the so-called "*valse des ministères*" [ministers' waltz]) following the fall of Jules Ferry, stormy elections, and the rise of Boulangisme. Freud rarely identified the objectives of political demonstrators; what he saw was mob behavior as such, something to become all too familiar again in Vienna a decade later: "The people seem to me of a different species from ourselves; I feel they are possessed of a thousand demons....I hear them yelling '*A la lanterne*' ['To the lamppost'] and '*à bas*' ['Down with...'] this man and that. I don't think they know the meaning of shame or fear....They are people given to psychical epidemics, historical mass convulsions, and they haven't changed since Victor Hugo wrote *Notre-Dame*."[14]

To the awe of the Church and the fear of the feverish crowd one must add one more perspective to triangulate Freud's Paris: the theater, and especially its women. Freud went to theater first in hopes of improving his French, found he understood little, but returned ever again for other reasons. Freud devoted one of the longest of his long letters to a scene-by-scene account of Sarah Bernhardt's performance in Victorien Sardou's melodrama, *Théodora*.[15] He was utterly bewitched by her portrayal of the Byzantine heroine, a prostitute become Empress: "...Her caressing and pleading, the postures she assumes, the way she wraps herself around a man, the way she acts with every limb, every joint—it's incredible. A remarkable creature, and I can imagine she is no different in life from what she is on the stage."

"For the sake of historical truth," Freud continues, "let us add that I again had to pay for this pleasure with an attack of migraine." The tensions of

---

13   Freud, *Dreams*, 506–507.
14   Freud to Minna Bernays, Paris, 3 Dec. 1885, *Letters*, 187–188.
15   Freud to Martha Bernays, Paris, 8 Nov. 1885; ibid., 178–182.

the Paris experience, his new receptivity, sensual as well as intellectual, to the realm of instinct were doubtless related to Freud's long separation from his Martha. He cheerfully admitted to her his frequent recourse to cocaine to keep his tensions down or his spirits up. While he surely concealed no actions from her, he revealed one fantasy—that he might marry the attractive daughter of Dr. Charcot and thus in one stroke solve his problems of power—professional, social, and sexual—that evidently evoked a nettled response from Martha, who could not take it as lightly as Freud tried to present it.[16] One suspects that the decorous Freud could not and did not reveal the full extent of his newfound feelings. They are perhaps better expressed in a joke he delighted to record at a later time, when he had discovered that jokes contain the expression of repressed wishes: A married couple is discussing the future. The man says to his wife: "If one of us should die, I shall go to Paris."[17]

In one of Freud's remarkable Paris letters, the very imagery he used seems to bring all the dimensions of his Paris experience into relation to the impact of Jean Martin Charcot: "I think I am changing a great deal.... Charcot, who is one of the greatest of physicians, and a man whose common sense borders on genius, is simply wrecking all my aims and opinions. I sometimes come out of his lectures as from out of Notre Dame," our militant anti-Catholic continues, "with an entirely new idea of perfection....It is three whole days since I have done any work, and I have no feelings of guilt," the erstwhile Puritan adds. "My brain is sated as after an evening in the theater. Whether the seed will ever bear fruit, I don't know; but I do know that no other human being has ever affected me in the same way....Or am I under the influence of this magically attractive and repulsive city?"[18]

Surely it was both. Paris, and Freud's quasi-stereotypical perception of it, provided the ideal setting to receive from Charcot a doctrine that opened the way to that questionable province of the psyche where neither body nor conscious mind seemed in control.

Before Freud left Paris for home he cemented his relations with Charcot

---

16   "Now just suppose I were not in love already and were something of an adventurer; it would be a strong temptation to court her [Mlle. Charcot], for nothing is more dangerous than a young girl bearing the features of a man whom one admires." Freud to Martha Bernays, Paris, 20 Jan. 1886, ibid., 196–197; 27 Jan. 1886, 197–198; 2 Feb. 1886, 201; 10 Feb. 1886, 206–207.

17   Freud, *Dreams*, 523.

18   Freud to Martha Bernays, Paris, 24 Nov. 1885, *Letters*, 184–185.

by volunteering as translator of a volume of his *Leçons sur les maladies du système nerveux* [*Lectures on the Diseases of the Nervous System,* 1883], including his lectures on hysteria. Thus Freud's tribute to English thought in his translation of John Stuart Mill's essay on the subjection of women found an appropriate French equivalent. Freud carried the symmetry into his family too: he named his firstborn son Jean Martin for Charcot, as he would soon, in tribute to Puritan England, name his second son Oliver, after Cromwell. Thus Freud's personal exemplars of English ego and Parisian id each had their namesakes among his children.

When Freud returned to Vienna he entered practice as a doctor of nervous diseases. He chose Easter Sunday to publish this good news in the *Neue Freie Presse.* Thus the Jewish admirer of Notre Dame combined an announcement of his own resurrection and new life with a defiance of Catholic sensibilities worthy of a Puritan prophet. Such were the extreme polarities which entered into the genesis of psychoanalysis.

III

By this time, you must be wondering whether the pictures that I have drawn of England and Paris justify my subtitle, "The Psycho-archeology of Civilizations." Since they antedate Freud's interests in either the depths of the psyche or archeology, our materials thus far have dealt with conscious ideas and values, not with buried ones; with the day-world, not the night-world. What is striking is the sharpness of the contrast between Freud's images of the two cultures. He not only kept their identities separate and antithetical but sought in neither any trace of the features he saw in the other. The Puritan-rationalist spectacles he wore when he looked at England allowed him to see there nothing of the cathedrals, crowds, or women that so caught his eye in France; nor did he remark the gracious, aristocratic side of English life and manners. In France, on the other hand, the image of the female and the Sphinx so dominated his perception that the positivist, rationalist, masculine side of French bourgeois society scarcely entered his field of vision. Finally, Freud made no attempt to establish any relationship between the contrasting values that attracted him in English and French culture. This he was to accomplish only indirectly in his encounter with Rome, where male and female, ethics and aesthetics—in short, the ego-world of London and the id-world of Paris—converged in bewildering conflation.

Rome had engaged Freud's fancy on and off since childhood. Not until the 1890s, when Freud was in his forties, while at work on *The Interpretation of Dreams,* did he conceive a truly passionate interest in the Eternal City. As in the early 1880s, when he had contemplated escape to the refuge of England, he entered in the mid-1890s another, deeper professional crisis. Where the impasse of the 1890s applied only to his career opportunities, the new one involved, by virtue of the very depth of his frustration, Freud's personal identity and intellectual direction as well.

I have elsewhere tried to show how the seething crisis of Austrian society, in which liberalism lacked the power to sustain itself against the rising tide of Catholic and nationalist anti-Semitic movements, affected Freud.[19] It drove him into social withdrawal as a Jew, into intellectual isolation as a scientist, and into introspection as a thinker. The more his outer life was mired, however, the more winged his ideas became. In his fundamental work, *The Interpretation of Dreams,* Freud transformed the poison of social frustration as Jew and as scientist into the elixir of psychological illumination. Essential to his procedure was to plumb the depths of his own personal history, thus to find a universal psychological structure, a key to human destiny that would transcend the collective history which until then had seemed to shape man's fate. Freud devised psychoanalysis as a counter-political theory in a situation of political despair. Where he had once been tempted to withdraw to England, he now turned inward into himself, to face and overcome the conflicts between his wishes and his hostile environment, by means of psychoanalysis as *theory.* As he did so, he also resolved, by means of psychoanalysis as *therapy,* the conflicts between his wishes and his values.

It was in the context of working through this intellectual and personal crisis that Freud's interest in antiquity and in Rome arose. He hit upon the analogy between his own procedure of digging into his own buried past as depth psychologist and the work of the archeologist. Soon his mild interest developed into an insatiable passion. He eagerly read the biography of Heinrich Schliemann, who fulfilled a childhood wish by his discovery of Troy. He began the collection of ancient artifacts that soon graced his office in the Berggasse. And, especially rare in those days of his social withdrawal, Freud made a new friend: Emanuel Löwy, a professor of archeology. "He

---

19   Carl E. Schorske, *Fin-de-siècle Vienna. Politics and Culture* (New York: Vintage, 1980), ch. 4. Unless otherwise indicated, what follows is based on the materials there presented.

keeps me up until three o'clock in the morning," Freud wrote to his dearest friend; "he tells me about Rome."[20]

What could be more natural than that Freud, an inveterate traveler, should pursue his newfound interest by visiting the Eternal City? But he found he could not. Five times Freud journeyed to Italy between 1895 and 1898, without ever reaching Rome. Some inhibition held him back. At the same time, the yearning to visit it grew ever more torturesome. Rome became literally the city of his dreams, and Freud began to speak of his longing for Rome as "deeply neurotic."[21] As such, he incorporated it into his self-analysis and into *The Interpretation of Dreams.*

Freud explored fully only one dimension of his Rome neurosis in *The Interpretation,* that which bore on his relations with his father. But in it he revealed also the centrality of the Jewish problem and Austrian politics in his own life. He recalled from his school days his hero-worship for Hannibal. "Like so many boys of that age, I had sympathized in the Punic Wars not with the Romans, but the Carthaginians. And when in the higher classes I began to understand for the first time what it meant to belong to an alien race, and anti-Semitic feelings among the other boys warned me that I must take a definite position, the figure of the Semitic general rose still higher in my esteem. To my youthful mind, Hannibal and Rome symbolized the conflict between the tenacity of Jewry and the organization of the Catholic church." Freud then recaptured an episode from his childhood where his father told him of having been insulted by Christians, without fighting back. Freud resented his father's "unheroic conduct." He remembered having wished that his father had enjoined him, as Hannibal's had, "to take vengeance on the Romans." Ever since that time, Freud reported, Hannibal had had a place in his fantasies. In the face of the newly threatening power of anti-Semitism in the 1890s, Freud interpreted his longing for Rome as "actually following in Hannibal's footsteps. Like him, I had been fated not to see Rome."[22]

Two aspects of Freud's interpretation of his Hannibal identification deserve notice: First, that he had the same attitude toward Christian Rome

20   Freud to Wilhelm Fliess, Vienna, 5 Nov. 1897, Sigmund Freud, *The Origins of Psychoanalysis. Letters, Drafts and Notes to Wilhelm Fliess, 1887–1902,* eds. Marie Bonaparte, Anna Freud, Ernst Kris; trans. Eric Mosbacher and James Strachey (New York: Doubleday Anchor Book, 1957), 232.

21   Freud to Fliess, Vienna, 3 Dec. 1897, ibid., 239.

22   Freud, *Dreams,* 229–230.

that the English Puritans had had, as the hated center of Catholic power; second, that he had taken on the paternal burden of defender of Jewish dignity, which, despite his anger at his father's impotence, he was himself now powerless to realize. Freud's Rome neurosis, his inability to reach the city, was from this perspective the consequence of guilt, of an undischarged obligation at once filial and political.

Yet Freud's actual dreams of Rome in the years 1896 and 1897 spoke a different language, one more akin to the seductive allure of his Paris than to the Puritan probity of his England. All of them suggest fulfillment rather than outright conquest. All conflate images of Catholic Rome with Jewish ideas and situations.[23] In one dream Rome appears as "the promised land seen from afar," implying Freud to be in the same relation to Rome as Moses to Israel. The vision, though Freud does not say so, seems to express a forbidden wish: a longing for an assimilation to the gentile world that his strong waking conscience—and even his dream-censor—would deny him. He also identifies Rome with Carlsbad, Bohemia's equivalent of our Palm Springs, a city of pleasure, rest, and cure; in short, an earthly city of recreation (re-creation), of resurrection. Freud compares himself in the analysis of this dream to a poor, gentle Jewish character in one of the Yiddish stories he loved so well. Because the little Jew did not have the train fare to Carlsbad, the conductor beat him up at every station; but, undaunted, he continued on his *via dolorosa* (the expression is Freud's). Thus the lofty vision of Moses-Freud seeing Israel-Rome "from afar" had its lowly analogue in the picture of the little-Jew-Christ-Freud reaching Carlsbad-Rome on a *via dolorosa*. A third dream reinforces the Christian theme but telescopes it into that of ancient, pagan Rome. From a train window Freud sees across the Tiber the Castel Sant'Angelo, at once papal castle and Roman imperial tomb. Tantalizingly, the train moves off before he can cross the Bridge of the Holy Angel to reach the castle—a house of both buried paganism and Christian salvation.

How different is the Rome of Freud the youth of the 1860s and 1870s—forbidding, hostile, bureaucratic—from this Rome of the dreaming man in the 1890s: the first an object of hate, to be destroyed, the second an object

---

23   Ibid., 226–229. One later Rome dream, in which the city is the setting of grief, is not included here. This dream's bearing on Freud's problem of ambivalence as Jew has been interestingly demonstrated by Peter Loewenberg in "A Hidden Zionist Theme in Freud's 'My Son, the Myops...' Dream," *Journal of the History of Ideas*, 31:129–132 (1970).

of desire, to be entered in love! Surely in the second of these Romes, we can descry the positive features of Freud's Paris: the awesome but glorious feminine Catholic spirit of Notre Dame, the allure of the city of pleasure (Carlsbad-Paris-Rome); in short, Mother and temptress at once. Indeed Freud provided, though not in *The Interpretation of Dreams,* the materials to connect the lure of Rome to his surrogate mother, a beloved Czech Nanny of his childhood. She had taught him about her Catholic faith and taken him to Church on Easter Sunday. In contrast to his father, she had given him "a high opinion of my own capacities." As the Rome of Hannibal was masculine, connected by Freud with his social duty and his oedipal conflict, so the Rome of Nanny was feminine, that of Mother Church, of tabooed oedipal love.[24]

While Freud in his psycho-archeological report analyzes only the first, pagan Rome, identifying with Hannibal and his wish "to take vengeance on the Romans," he gives us a clue that opens still another road that leads, like that of Nanny, to a Rome more consonant with the dream-wishes to enter it in love and fulfillment. The clue lies in a quotation from a German author which occurred to Freud in the course of wrestling with his Rome neurosis: "Which of...two [men] paced his study in greater excitement after forming his plan to go to Rome: Winckelmann or Hannibal?" Freud unequivocally answered for himself, "Hannibal," for he had been "fated not to see Rome." But Winckelmann would correspond to the other side of Freud's dream-truth, the one he failed to analyze for us. For Winckelmann, the great archeologist and art historian, had much in common with Freud: his poverty; an acute sense of low social origins; failure to find for many years a congenial position or professional recognition; a series of intense male friendships with homosexual overtones; hatred of political tyranny; hostility to organized religion; and a generativity crisis at the age of 40 that resulted, like Freud's, in a "first work" of a new and revolutionary kind. Above all, Winckelmann, a Protestant, overcame his scruples and embraced Catholicism in order to enter Rome, to be able to pursue his passion for classical antiquity. He conquered his conscience for the sake of his science, his *amor intellectualis* [intellectual love] for Rome.

Was not Freud more scientist than general—and a "soft" scientist at that?

---

24   Freud to Fliess, Vienna, 3–4 Oct. 1897; Vienna, 15 Oct. 1897, *Origins,* 221–228. The most comprehensive treatment of the Nanny and Freud's Rome neurosis is Kenneth A. Grigg, "'All Roads Lead to Rome': The Role of the Nursemaid in Freud's Dreams," *Journal of the American Psychoanalytic Association,* 21: 108–126 (1973).

Was he not, on his journey to Rome, following in Winckelmann's footsteps rather than in Hannibal's? Freud's passionate cleaving to the friendship of Wilhelm Fliess as sole intellectual confidant during these years of crisis had homoerotic overtones that speak for Winckelmann too. Fliess was even more radically committed to the primacy of sexuality in psychic life than Freud. He advanced a radical theory of bisexuality which Freud seriously entertained. (Paris, where Freud espoused Charcot's theory that males too could suffer from the woman's malady, hysteria, had prepared him for that.) Freud called their series of meetings à *deux* "congresses"; he particularly longed for a congress on classical soil. When Fliess proposed in 1901 that they hold their congress at Easter, Freud replied that he was "powerfully gripped" *(mächtig gepackt)* by the idea; but since the friendship was then nearing its end, Freud declined.[25] He could not but admit to Fliess the pull of Rome as goal, as scene of resurrection: "In the midst of this mental and material depression, I am haunted by the thought of spending Easter week in Rome this year. Not that there is any justification for it—I have achieved nothing yet." Or again: "I shall no more get to Rome this Easter than you will."[26]

Of course, Freud was not ready to go the course of Winckelmann, to join the Church of Rome. The Hannibal and the Cromwell in him—the Jewish, liberal, and Anglophile values that furnished his conscience by day and censored his dreams by night—assured his capacity to resist any such apostasy. But the temptation which Winckelmann had embraced in Rome, so like the one that Freud had encountered in Paris—the affective power of Eros with which Catholic Rome was associated—Freud recognized as a deeper reality in his own psyche. It was his glory to exhume it painfully in himself and then to put it to work in building his dynamic psychoanalytic system.

After Freud finished his self-analysis and *The Interpretation of Dreams* in 1900, the gates of Rome opened to him at last. He entered the city not "to take vengeance on the Romans," nor to yield to the temptation of Holy Mother Church, but as an intellectual pilgrim. "It was an overwhelming experience for me, the fulfillment of a long-cherished wish," he wrote to Fliess. "It was also," he added, "slightly disappointing." Though he did not find all the strata of Rome's symbolic meaning for his psychic life simultaneously present, as

---

25   Freud to Fliess, Vienna, 23 March 1901, *Origins*, 315-316.
26   Freud to Fliess, Vienna, 30 Jan.; Vienna, 15 Feb. 1901, ibid., 328-329.

in the metaphor with which this paper began, Freud could distinguish three Romes clearly, by historical period. Taking them in inverse order, the third Rome, modern Rome, was "hopeful and likeable." The second, Catholic Rome, with its "lie of salvation," was "disturbing," making him "incapable of putting out of my mind my own misery and all the other misery which I know to exist." Was not his misery the result of the powerful attraction of the Catholic world of Notre Dame, and the temptation of professional salvation through conversion after the example of Winckelmann—all of which conflicted with his Old Testament conscience and his ethnic fidelity? But beneath these, there was the first Rome, the Rome of antiquity. It alone moved him to deep enthusiasm: "I could have worshipped the humble and mutilated remnants of the Temple of Minerva."[27]

Minerva? A true brainchild of her father Jupiter, she was at once the goddess of disposing wisdom and protectrix of the polis. Her statue was just then (1902) being placed before Vienna's Parliament building, as the belated symbol of the liberal-rationalist polity. Minerva was also a phallic female, an anti-erotic goddess, who repelled her enemies with her spear, her snaky aegis, and her gorgon-studded shield. She unified in her ascetic bisexuality and rational cool the civic spirit that had so attracted Freud to masculine England with the female beauty and irrational power that had so moved him in Paris. In the deepest, pagan layer of the Eternal City, where he found the mutilated remnants of Minerva, Freud the psycho-archeologist could celebrate his own achievement: to reconcile in thought the polarities of male and female, conscience and instinct, ego and id, Jewish patriarchy and Catholic maternalism, London and Paris—all in the name of science. Freud's solution to his own problem with many-layered Rome brought with it the restoration of his own ego, endowing it with the capacity to comprehend a contradictory and nonhomogeneous reality and thus to find a way to live with it.

27   Freud to Fliess, [Vienna], 19 Sept. 1901, ibid., 336.

FREUD AND MORAL REFLECTION
by Richard Rorty

The mechanical mind: Hume and Freud

Freud thought of himself as part of the same "decentering" movement of thought to which Copernicus and Darwin belonged. In a famous passage, he says that psychoanalysis "seeks to prove to the ego that it is not even master in its own house, but must content itself with scanty information of what is going on unconsciously in its mind." He compares this with the realization that "our earth was not the center of the universe but only a tiny fragment of a cosmic system of scarcely imaginable vastness" and with the discovery, by Darwin, of our "ineradicable animal nature."[1]

Copernicus, Darwin, and Freud do have something important in common, but Freud does not give us a clear idea of what that is. It is not evident that successive decenterings add up to a history of humiliation; Copernicus and Darwin might claim that by making God and the angels less plausible, they have left human beings on top of the heap. The suggestion that we have discovered, humiliatingly, that humanity is less important than we had thought is not perspicuous. For it is not clear what "importance" can mean in this context. Further, the claim that psychoanalysis has shown that the ego is not master in its own house is unhelpful, for the relevant sense of "mastery" is unclear. Does our sense of our importance, or our capacity for self-control, really depend on the belief that we are transparent to ourselves? Why should the discovery of the unconscious add humiliation to the discovery of the passions?

I think one gets a better idea of the similarity Freud was trying to describe

---

1   *The Standard Edition of the Complete Psychological Works of Sigmund Freud*, trans. James Strachey (London: Hogarth Press, 1966), 16:284–285. Future references to Freud will be to this edition (abbreviated *S. E.*), and will be inserted in the text.

by contrasting a world of natural kinds with a world of machines—a world of Aristotelian substances with a world of homogenous particles combining and disassociating according to universal laws. Think of the claim that "man is a natural kind" not as saying that human beings are at the center of something, but that they *have* a center, in a way that a machine does not. A substance that exemplifies an Aristotelian natural kind divides into a central essence—one that provides a built-in purpose—and a set of peripheral accidents. But an artifact's formal and final causes may be distinct; the same machine, for example, may be used for many different purposes. A machine's purpose is not built in.[2] If humanity is a natural kind, then perhaps we can find our center and so learn how to live well. But if we are machines, then it is up to us to invent a use for ourselves. What was decisive about the Copernican Revolution was not that it moved us human beings from the center of the universe, but that it began, in Dyksterhuis's phrase, the "mechanization of the world picture."[3] Copernicus and Newton between them made it hard to think of the universe as an edifying spectacle. When an infinite universe of pointless corpuscles replaced a closed world, it became hard to imagine what it would be like to look down upon

---

2   There can be such a thing as a "purer" Aristotelian substance—one that realizes its essence better because it is less subject to irrelevant accidental changes. (Indeed, Aristotle arranges substances in a hierarchy according to their degree of materiality, their degree of susceptibility to such changes—a hierarchy with "pure actuality" at the top.) But there is no such thing as a purified machine, though there may be another machine that accomplishes the same purpose more efficiently. Machines have no centers to which one can strip them down; stripped-down versions of machines are different machines, machines for doing or producing different things, nor more perfect versions of the same machine.

3   The Copernican model of the heavens could not have been accepted without also accepting the corpuscularian mechanics of Galileo and Descartes. Their mechanics was the entering wedge for a Newtonian paradigm of scientific explanation—one that predicted events on the basis of a universal homogenous microstructure, rather than revealing the different natures of the various natural kinds. The reason why "the new philosophy" cast all in doubt was not that people felt belittled when the sun took the place of the earth but that it had become hard to see what, given Galilean space, could be meant by the universe having a center. As it became harder to know what a God's-eye view would be like, it became harder to believe in God. As it became harder to think of the common-sense way of breaking up the world into "natural" kinds as more than a practical convenience, it became harder to make sense of the Aristotelian essence/accident distinction. So the very idea of the "nature" of something as setting the standards that things of that sort ought to fulfill began to blur.

the Creation and find it good.[4] The universe began to look like a rather simple, boring machine, rambling off beyond the horizon, rather than like a bounded and well-composed tableau. So the idea of a center no longer seemed applicable. Analogously, the result of Darwin's and Mendel's mechanization of biology was to set aside an edifying hierarchy of natural kinds. Viewing the various species of plants and animals as the temporary results of interactions between fortuitous environmental pressure and random mutations made the world of living creatures as pointless as Newtonian mechanics had made cosmology. Mechanization meant that the world in which human beings lived no longer taught them anything about how they should live.

In trying to see how Freud fits into this story of decentering-as-mechanization, one should begin by noting that Freud was not the first to suggest that, having mechanized everything else, we mechanize the mind as well. Hume had already treated ideas and impressions not as properties of a substratal self but as mental atoms whose arrangement *was* the self. This arrangement was determined by laws of association, analogues of the law of gravitation. Hume thought of himself as the Newton of the mind, and the mechanical mind he envisaged was—viewed from above, so to speak—just as morally pointless as Newton's corpuscularian universe.

Hume, however, suggested that the mechanization of neither nature nor the mind mattered for purposes of finding a self-image. With a sort of proto-pragmatist insouciance, he thought that talk about the atoms of

---

4   In particular, it became difficult to see what the point of *man* could be—difficult to preserve anything like Aristotle's "functional" concept of man, well described by Alasdair MacIntyre as follows: "Moral arguments within the classical, Aristotelian tradition—whether in its Greek or its medieval versions—involve at least one central functional concept, the concept of *man* understood as having an essential nature and an essential purpose or function. Aristotle takes it as a starting-point for ethical inquiry that the relationship of 'man' to 'living well' is analogous to that of 'harpist' to 'playing the harp well'....But the use of 'man' as a functional concept is far older than Aristotle and it does not initially derive from Aristotle's metaphysical biology. It is rooted in the forms of a social life in which the theorists of the classical tradition give expression. For according to that tradition, to be a man is to fill a set of roles, each of which has its own point and purpose: a member of a family, a citizen, soldier, philosopher, servant of God. It is only when man is thought of as an individual prior to and apart from all roles that 'man' ceases to be a functional concept." (MacIntyre, *After Virtue* [Notre Dame, Ind.: Notre Dame University Press, 1981], 56; subsequent page references in main text). I take up MacIntyre's suggestion that we need to recapture such a concept in the final section of this essay.

Democritus, Newton's shining lights, and his own "impressions and ideas" offered, at most, a handy way of describing things and people for purposes of predicting and controlling them. For moral purposes, for purposes of seeing life as having a point, such talk might be irrelevant. Like Blake, Hume was prepared to say that the view from above—the view of the Baconian predictor and controller—was irrelevant to our sense of centeredness. His pragmatical reconciliation of freedom and determinism, like his reconciliation of armchair skepticism with theoretical curiosity and practical benevolence, is an invitation to take the mechanization of the mind lightly—as no more than an intriguing intellectual exercise, the sort of thing that a young person might do in order to become famous.

It is tempting to respond to Freud in the same way that Hume responded to his own mechanizing efforts: to say that for purposes of moral reflection a knowledge of Freudian unconscious motivation is as irrelevant as a knowledge of Humean associations or of neurophysiology. But this response is unconvincing. Unlike Hume, Freud *did* change our self-image. Finding out about our unconscious motives is not just an intriguing exercise, but more like a moral obligation. What difference between Hume's and Freud's ways of extending mechanization to the mind accounts for Freud's relevance to our moral consciousness?

If one views Freud's dictum that the ego is not master in its own house as saying merely that we often act in ways that could not have been predicted on the basis of our introspectible beliefs and desires, Freud will be merely reiterating a commonplace of Greek thought. If one views it as the claim that the mind can, for purposes of prediction and control, be treated as a set of associative mechanisms, a realm in which there are no accidents, Freud will be saying little that Hume had not said. So one must find another interpretation. One gets a clue, I think, from the fact that the phrase "not even master in its own house" is to the point only if some other person is behaving as if he or she were in charge. The phrase is an appropriate response to the incursion of an unwanted guest—for example, to the onset of schizophrenia. But it is not an appropriate reaction, for example, to an explanation of the dependence of our mood on our endocrine system. For glands are not, so to speak, quasi people with whom to struggle. Nor are neurons, which is why the possible identity of the mind with the brain is of no moral interest. Physiological discoveries can tell us how to predict and control ourselves—including how to predict and control our beliefs and desires—without threatening or changing our self-image. For such discoveries do not suggest that we are being shouldered aside by somebody else.

Psychological mechanisms will seem more decentering than physiological mechanisms only if one is of a naturally metaphysical turn of mind, insistent on pressing the questions, "But what am I *really*? What is my *true* self? What is *essential* to me?" Descartes and Kant had this sort of mind and so, in our day, do reductionist metaphysicians such as B. F. Skinner and antireductionist champions of "subjectivity" and "phenomenology" such as Thomas Nagel and Richard Wollheim. But the mechanization of nature made proto-pragmatists of most people, allowing them to shrug off questions of essence. They became accustomed to speaking one sort of language for Baconian purposes of prediction and control and another for purposes of moral reflection. They saw no need to raise the question of which language represented the world or the self as it is "in itself."[5] Yet Freudian discoveries are troubling even for pragmatists. Unlike the atoms of Democritus or Hume, the Freudian unconscious does not look like something that we might usefully, to achieve certain of our purposes, describe ourselves as. It looks like somebody who is stepping into our shoes, somebody who has different purposes than we do. It looks like a person using us rather than a thing we can use.

This clue—the fact that psychological mechanisms look most disturbing and decentering when they stop looking like mechanisms and start looking like persons—has been followed up by Donald Davidson. In a remarkable essay called "Paradoxes of Irrationality," Davidson notes that philosophers have always been upset by Freud's insistence on "partitioning" the self. They have tended to reject Freud's threatening picture of quasi selves

---

5   Nonintellectuals' conviction that what the intellectuals talk about does not really matter was greatly strengthened when the new Enlightenment intellectuals informed them that the previous batch of intellectuals—the priests—had been *completely* wrong. One consequence of the mechanization of nature, and of the resulting popularity of a pragmatic, Baconian attitude toward knowledge-claims, was a heightened cynicism and indifference about the questions that intellectuals discuss. This is why metaphysical issues about "the nature of reality" and "the true self" have less resonance and popular appeal than religious heresies once did, and why philosophical questions raised within Comte's "positive," postmetaphysical perspective have even less. People always thought the priests a bit funny, but also a bit awe-inspiring. They thought German idealists, and Anglo-Saxon positivists, *merely* funny. By contrast, they take psychoanalysts seriously enough to attempt to imitate them, as in the development of parlor analysis and of psychobabble.

lurking beneath the threshold of consciousness as an unnecessarily vivid way of describing the incoherence and confusion that may afflict a single self. They hope thereby to remain faithful to the commonsense assumption that a single human body typically contains a single self. Davidson defends Freudian partitioning by pointing out that there is no reason to say "You unconsciously believe that p" rather than "There is something within you which causes you to act as if you believed that p," unless one is prepared to round out the characterization of the unconscious quasi self who "believes that p" by ascribing a host of other beliefs (mostly true, and mostly consistent with p) to that quasi self. One can only attribute a belief to something if one simultaneously attributes lots of other mostly true and mostly consistent beliefs. Beliefs and desires, unlike Humean ideas and impressions, come in packages.[6]

Davidson puts these holistic considerations to work as follows. He identifies (not explicitly, but, if my reading of him is right, tacitly) being a person with being a coherent and plausible set of beliefs and desires. Then he points out that the force of saying that a human being sometimes behaves irrationally is that he or she sometimes exhibits behavior that cannot be explained by reference to a single such set. Finally, he concludes that the point of "partitioning" the self between a consciousness and an unconscious is that the latter can be viewed as an alternative set, inconsistent with the familiar set that we identify with consciousness, yet sufficiently coherent internally to count as a person. This strategy leaves open the possibility that the same human body can play host to two or more persons. These persons enter into causal relations with each other, as well as with the body whose movements are brought about by the beliefs and desires of one or the other of them. But they do not, normally, have conversational relations. That is, one's unconscious beliefs are not *reasons* for a change in one's conscious beliefs, but they may *cause* changes in the latter beliefs, just as may portions of one's body (e.g., the retina, the fingertips, the pituitary gland, the gonads).

To see the force of Davidson's suggestion is to appreciate the crucial difference between Hume and Freud. This is that Hume's mental atoms

---

6   Even if, as Hume thought, there is a possible universe consisting only of one sense-impression, we cannot make sense of the idea of a universe consisting only of the belief that, for example, Caesar crossed the Rubicon. Further, there is no such thing as an incoherent arrangement of Humean mental atoms. But there is such a thing as a set of beliefs and desires so incoherent that we cannot attribute them to a single self.

included only subpropositional components of beliefs—mostly names of perceptible and introspectible qualia. The mechanization of the self that Hume suggested, and that associationist psychology developed, amounted to little more than a transposition into mentalistic terminology of a rather crude physiology of perception and memory. By contrast, Freud populated inner space not with analogues of Boylean corpuscles but with analogues of persons—internally coherent clusters of belief and desire. Each of these quasi persons is, in the Freudian picture, a part of a single unified *causal* network, but not of a single person (since the criterion for individuation of a person is a certain minimal coherence among its beliefs and desires). Knowledge of all these persons is necessary to predict and control a human being's behavior (and in particular his or her "irrational" behavior), but only one of these persons will be available (at any given time) to introspection.

The rational unconscious as conversational partner

If one accepts this Davidsonian explanation of Freud's basic strategy, then one has taken a long step toward seeing why psychoanalysis can aptly be described as a decentering. For now one can see Freudian mechanisms as having, so to speak, a human interest that no physiological or Humean mechanism could have. One can see why it is hard to dismiss the Freudian unconscious as just one more useful, if paradoxical, redescription of the world that science has invented for purposes of saving the phenomena—the sort of redescription that can be ignored by everyday, practical purposes (as, for example, one ignores heliocentrism). The suggestion that some unknown persons are causing us (or, to stress the alienation produced by this suggestion, causing our bodies) to do things we would rather not do is decentering in a way that an account of heavenly bodies (or of the descent of man) is not. One will be thrown off base by this suggestion even if one has no interest in Aristotelian, metaphysical questions about one's "essence" or one's "true self." One can be entirely pragmatical in one's approach to life and still feel that something needs to be *done* in response to such a suggestion.

To take Freud's suggestion seriously is to wish to become acquainted with these unfamiliar persons, if only as a first step toward killing them off. This wish will take the place, for a pragmatical Freudian, of the religious and metaphysical desire to find one's "true center." It initiates a task that can plausibly be described as a moral obligation—the task whose goal is summed up in the phrase "where id was, there shall ego be." This goal does not require the Aristotelian notion that one's ego is more "natural" or more truly "oneself" than one's id. But adopting this goal does restore a point to the imperative "Know thyself," an imperative that one might have thought inapplicable to the self-as-machine.

On Freud's account of self-knowledge, what we are morally obligated to know about ourselves is not our essence, not a common human nature that is somehow the source and locus of moral responsibility. Far from being of what we share with the other members of our species, self-knowledge is precisely of what divides us from them: our accidental idiosyncrasies, the "irrational" components in ourselves, the ones that split us up into incompatible sets of beliefs and desires. The study of "the nature of the mind," construed as the study either of Humean association of ideas or of Freudian metapsychology, is as pointless, for purposes of moral reflection, as the study of the laws of celestial motion. What *is* of interest is the study of the idiosyncratic raw material whose processing Humean and Freudian mechanisms are postulated to predict, and of the idiosyncratic products of this processing. For only study of these concrete details will let us enter into conversational relations with our unconscious and, at the ideal limit of such conversation, let us break down the partitions.

The view of Freud that I am proposing will seem plausible only if one makes a clear distinction between two senses of "the unconscious": (1) a sense in which it stands for one or more well-articulated systems of beliefs and desires, systems that are just as complex, sophisticated, and internally consistent as the normal adult's conscious beliefs and desires; and (2) a sense in which it stands for a seething mass of inarticulate instinctual energies, a "reservoir of libido" to which consistency is irrelevant. In the second sense, the unconscious is just another name for "the passions," the lower part of the soul, the bad, false self. Had this been the only sense Freud gave to the term, his work would have left our strategies of character-development, and our self-image, largely unchanged. What is novel in Freud's view of the unconscious is his claim that our unconscious selves are not dumb, sullen, lurching brutes, but rather the intellectual peers of our conscious selves, possible conversational partners for those selves. As Rieff puts it, "Freud democratized genius by giving everyone a creative unconscious."[7]

---

7   Philip Rieff, *Freud: The Mind of the Moralist* (New York: Harper and Row, 1966), 36.

This suggestion that one or more clever, articulate, inventive persons are at work behind the scene—cooking up our jokes, inventing our metaphors, plotting our dreams, arranging our slips, and censoring our memories—is what grips the imagination of the lay reader of Freud. As Freud himself said, if psychoanalysis had stuck to the neuroses, it would never have attracted the attention of the intellectuals.[8] It was the application of psychoanalytical notions to normal life that first suggested that Freud's ideas might call for a revision in our self-image. For this application breaks the connection between the Platonic reason/passion distinction and the conscious/unconscious distinction. It substitutes a picture of sophisticated transactions between two or more "intellects" for the traditional picture of one "intellect" struggling with a mob of "irrational" brutes.

The Platonic tradition had thought of articulate beliefs—or, more generally, propositional attitudes—as the preserve of the higher part of the soul. It thought of the lower parts as "bodily," as animal-like, and in particular as prelinguistic. But a witty unconscious is necessarily a linguistic unconscious. Further, if "rational" means "capable of weaving complex, internally consistent, networks of belief" rather than "capable of contemplating reality as it is," then a witty unconscious is also a *rational* unconscious—one that can no more tolerate inconsistency than can consciousness.[9] So we need to distinguish the unconscious as "the deepest strata of our minds, made up of instinctual impulses," strata that know "nothing that is negative, and no negation," in which "contradictories coincide" (*S. E.* 14:296), from the unconscious as the sensitive, whacky, backstage partner who feeds us our best lines. The latter is somebody who has a well-worked-out, internally consistent view of the world—though one that may be hopelessly wrong on certain crucial points. One needs to distinguish Freud's banal claim that "our intellect is a feeble and dependent thing, a plaything and tool of

---

8   "The importance of psycho-analysis for psychiatry would never have drawn the attention of the intellectual world to it or won it a place in *The History of our Times*. This result was brought about by the relation of psycho-analysis to normal, not to pathological, mental life" (Freud, *S. E.* 19:205; see also 18:240). Even if analytic psychiatry should some day be abandoned in favor of chemical and microsurgical forms of treatment, the connections that Freud drew between such emotions as sexual yearning and hostility on the one hand, and between dreams and parapraxes on the other, would remain part of the common sense of our culture.

9   See Davidson, "Paradoxes of Irrationality," in *Philosophical Essays on Freud*, ed. R. Wollheim and J. Hopkins (Cambridge: Cambridge University Press, 1982), especially his discussion of "the paradox of rationality," 303.

our instincts and affects" (*S. E.* 14:301)—which is just a replay of Hume's claim that "reason is, and ought to be, the slave of the passions"[10]—from his interesting and novel claim that the conscious/unconscious distinction cuts across the human/animal and reason/instinct distinctions.

If one concentrates on the latter claim, then one can see Freud as suggesting that, on those occasions when we are tempted to complain that two souls dwell, alas, in our breast, we think of the two as one more-or-less sane and one more-or-less crazy human soul, rather than as one human soul and one bestial soul. On the latter, Platonic model, self-knowledge will be a matter of self-purification—of identifying our true, human self and expelling, curbing, or ignoring the animal self. On the former model, self-knowledge will be a matter of getting acquainted with one or more crazy quasi people, listening to their crazy accounts of how things are, seeing why they hold the crazy views they do, and learning something from them. It will be a matter of self-enrichment. To say "Where id was, there will ego be" will not mean "Whereas once I was driven by instinct, I shall become autonomous, motivated solely by reason." Rather, it will mean something like: "Once I could not figure out why I was acting so oddly, and hence wondered if I were, somehow, under the control of a devil or a beast. But now I shall be able to see my actions as rational, as making sense, though perhaps based on mistaken premises. I may even discover that those premises were not mistaken, that my unconscious knew better than I did."[11]

---

10   *Any* associationist psychology will make *that* claim. For it is a corollary of the claim that reason is not a faculty of contemplating essence but only a faculty of inferring beliefs from other beliefs. Since the initial premises of such inferences must then be supplied by something other than reason, and if the only faculty that can be relevantly opposed to "reason" is "passion," then Hume's claim follows trivially. But it would, of course, be more consistent with the mechanistic vocabulary of associationist psychology to drop talk of faculties and, in particular, to drop the terms "reason" and "passion." Once the mind becomes a machine instead of a quasi person, it no longer has faculties, much less higher and lower ones. Hume is interlacing the old vocabulary of faculties with the results of the new associationism for the sake of shock value.

11   This way of stating the aim of psychoanalytic treatment may seem to make everything sound too sweetly reasonable. It suggests that the analyst serves as a sort of moderator at a symposium: he or she introduces, for example, a consciousness which thinks that Mother is a long-suffering object of pity to an unconscious which thinks of her as a voracious seductress, letting the two hash out the pros and cons. It is of course true that the facts of resistance forbid the analyst to think in conversational terms. He or she must instead think in terms of Freud's various topographic-hydraulic models of libidinal flow, hoping to find in these models

The advantage of this way of thinking of the passions is that it enables one to take a similar view of conscience. For just as this view humanizes what the Platonic tradition took to be the urges of an animal, so it humanizes what that tradition thought of as divine inspiration. It makes conscience, like passion, one more set of human beliefs and desires—another story about how the world is, another Weltanschauung. Most important, it makes it *just* another story—not one that (in the case of the passions) is automatically suspect nor one that (in the case of conscience) is automatically privileged. It treats, so to speak, the three different stories told by the id, the superego, and the ego as alternative extrapolations from a common experience—in particular, experience of childhood events. Each story is an attempt to make these events coherent with later events, but the stimuli provided by such events are (usually) so diverse and confusing that no *single* consistent set of beliefs and desires is able to make them all hang together.

To view these three (or more) stories as on a par, as alternative explanations of a confusing situation, is part of what Rieff calls "Freud's egalitarian

---

suggestions about how to overcome resistance, what meaning to assign to novel symptoms, and so forth.

But it is also true that the patient has no choice but to think in conversational terms. (This is why self-analysis will usually not work, why treatment can often do what reflection cannot.) For purposes of the patient's conscious attempt to reshape his or her character, he or she cannot use a self-description in terms of cathexes, libidinal flow, and the like; topographic-hydraulic models cannot form part of one's self-image, any more than can a description of one's endocrine system. When the patient thinks about competing descriptions of his or her mother, the patient has to think dialectically, to grant that there is much to be said on both sides. To think, as opposed to react to a new stimulus, simply *is* to compare and contrast candidates for admission into one's set of beliefs and desires. So, while the analyst is busy thinking causally, in terms of the patient's reactions to stimuli (and in particular the stimuli that occur while the patient is on the couch), the patient has to think of his or her unconscious as, at least potentially, a conversational partner.

These two ways of thinking seem to me alternative tools, useful for different purposes, rather than contradictory claims. I do not think (despite the arguments of, for example, Paul Ricoeur and Roy Schafer) that there is a tension in Freud's thought between "energetics" and "hermeneutics." Rather, the two seem to me to be as compatible as, for example, microstructural and macrostructural descriptions of the same object (e.g., Eddington's table). But to defend my eirenic attitude properly I should offer an account of "resistance" that chimes with Davidson's interpretation of the unconscious, and I have not yet figured out how to do this. (I am grateful to George Thomas, Seymour Rabinowitz, and Cecil Cullender for pointing out this difficulty to me.)

revision of the traditional idea of an hierarchical human nature."[12] To adopt a self-image that incorporates this egalitarian revision is to think that there is no single right answer to the question "What *did* happen to me in the past?" It is also to think that there is no such answer to the question "What sort of person am I now?" It is to recognize that the choice of a vocabulary in which to describe either one's childhood or one's character cannot be made by inspecting some collection of "neutral facts" (e.g., a complete videotape of one's life history). It is to give up the urge to purification, to achieve a stripped-down version of the self, and to develop what Rieff calls "tolerance of ambiguities...the key to what Freud considered the most difficult of all personal accomplishments: a genuinely stable character in an unstable time."[13] On the view I am offering, Freud gave us a new technique for achieving a genuinely stable character: the technique of lending a sympathetic ear to our own tendencies to instability, by creating them as alternative ways of making sense of the past, ways that have as good a claim on our attention as do the familiar beliefs and desires that are available to introspection. His mechanistic view of the self gave us a vocabulary that lets us describe all the various parts of the soul, conscious and unconscious alike, in homogenous terms: as equally plausible candidates for "the true self."

But to say that all the parts of the soul are equally plausible candidates is to discredit both the idea of a "true self" and the idea of "the true story about how things are." It is to view the enlightened, liberated self—the self that has finally succeeded in shaping itself—as a self that has given up the need to "see things steadily and see them whole," to penetrate beyond shifting appearances to a constant reality. Maturity will, according to this view, consist rather in an ability to seek out new redescriptions of one's own past—an ability to take a nominalistic, ironic view of oneself. By turning the Platonic parts of the soul into conversational partners for one another, Freud did for the variety of interpretations of each person's past what the Baconian approach to science and philosophy did for the variety of descriptions of the universe as a whole. He let us see alternative narratives and alternative vocabularies as instruments for change, rather than as candidates for a correct depiction of how things are in themselves.

---

12   Philip Rieff, *The Triumph of the Therapeutic* (New York: Harper and Row, 1966), 56.
13   Ibid., 57.

Much of what I have been saying is summarized in Freud's remark, "If one considers chance to be unworthy of determining our fate, it is simply a relapse into the pious view of the Universe which Leonardo himself was on the way to overcoming when he wrote that the sun does not move" (*S. E.* XI:137).[14] This recommendation that we see chance as "not unworthy of determining our fate" has as a corollary that we see ourselves as having the beliefs and emotions we do, including our (putatively) "specifically moral" beliefs and emotions, because of some very particular, idiosyncratic things that have happened in the history of the race, and to ourselves in the course of growing up. Such a recognition produces the ability to be Baconian about oneself. It lets one see oneself as a Rube Goldberg machine that requires much tinkering, rather than as a substance with a precious essence to be discovered and cherished. It produces what Whitehead called "the virtues which Odysseus shares with the foxes"—rather than, for example, those which Achilles shares with the lions, or those which Plato and Aristotle hoped to share with the gods.

From this Baconian angle, the point of psychoanalysis is the same as that of reflection on the sort of character one would like to have, once one ceases to take a single vocabulary for granted and begins the attempt to revise and enlarge the very vocabulary in which one is at present reflecting. The point of both exercises is to find new self-descriptions whose adoption will enable one to alter one's behavior. Finding out the views of one's unconscious about one's past is a way of getting some additional suggestions about how to describe (and change) oneself in the future. As a way of getting such suggestions, psychoanalysis differs from reading history, novels, or treatises on moral philosophy only in being more painful, in being more likely to produce radical change, and in requiring a partner.

Purification and self-enlargement

Because morality is associated both with human solidarity and with tragedy, my claim that attention to personal idiosyncrasy "remoralizes" a mechanistic self may seem paradoxical. One might protest, in the spirit of Kant, that the whole point of morality is self-forgetfulness, not making an exception

---

14   It is interesting that in the passage cited Freud is referring back to a passage (*S. E.* XI:76) where he credits Leonardo not only with anticipating Copernicus but with having "divined the history of the stratification and fossilization in the Arno Valley," a suggestion Leonardo anticipated Lyell (and so, in a way, Darwin) as well.

of oneself, seeing oneself as counting for no more than any other human being, being motivated by what is common to all humanity. To emphasize idiosyncrasy is to emphasize the comic variety of human life rather than the tragedies that morality hopes to avert.

The appearance of paradox results from the fact that "morality" can mean either the attempt to be just in one's treatment of others or the search for perfection in oneself. The former is public morality, codifiable in statutes and maxims. The latter is private morality, the development of character. Like Freud, I am concerned only with the latter. Morality as the search for justice swings free of religion, science, metaphysics, and psychology. It is the relatively simple and obvious side of morality—the part that nowadays, in the wake of Freud, is often referred to as "culture" or "repression." This is the side of morality that instructs us to tell the truth, avoid violence, eschew sex with near relations, keep our promises, and abide by the Golden Rule.

The story of progress in public morality is largely irrelevant to the story of the mechanization of the world view.[15] Galileo, Darwin, and Freud did little to help or hinder such progress. They have nothing to say in answer either to the Athenian question "Does justice pay?" or to the Californian question "How much repression need I endure?" Freud, in particular, has no contribution to make to social theory. His domain is the portion of morality that cannot be identified with "culture"; it is the private life, the search for a character, the attempt of individuals to be reconciled with themselves (and, in the case of some exceptional individuals, to make their lives works of art).[16]

---

15 The Enlightenment attempt to connect the two by seeing both feudalism and Aristotelian science as instances of "prejudice and superstition" was a self-deceptive neo-Aristotelian attempt to preserve the idea of man as an animal whose essence is rationality, while simultaneously identifying rationality with certain newly created institutions.

16 Here I am agreeing with Rieff against, for example, Fromm and Marcuse: "Psychoanalysis is the doctrine of the private man defending himself against public encroachment. He cultivates the private life and its pleasures, and if he does take part in public affairs it is for consciously private motives" (Rieff, *The Mind of the Moralist*, 278). Rieff seems to me right in saying that Freud had little to say about how and whether society might be made "less repressive": "Like those who worked for shorter hours but nevertheless feared what men might do with their leisure, Freud would have welcomed more constructive releases from our stale moralities, but did not propose to substitute a new one. Our private ethics were his scientific problem: he had no new public ethics to suggest, no grand design for the puzzle of our common life'" (ibid., 38).

Such an attempt can take one of two antithetical forms: a search for purity or a search for self-enlargement. The ascetic life commended by Plato and criticized by Nietzsche is the paradigm of the former. The "aesthetic" life criticized by Kierkegaard is the paradigm of the latter. The desire to purify oneself is the desire to slim down, to peel away everything that is accidental, to will one thing, to intensify, to become a simpler and more transparent being. The desire to enlarge oneself is the desire to embrace more and more possibilities, to be constantly learning, to give oneself over entirely to curiosity, to end by having envisaged all the possibilities of the past and of the future. It was the goal shared by, for example, de Sade, Byron, and Hegel.[17] On the view I am presenting, Freud is an apostle of this aesthetic life, the life of unending curiosity, the life that seeks to extend its own bounds rather than to find its center.

For those who decline the options offered by de Sade and Byron (sexual experimentation, political engagement), the principal technique of self-enlargement will be Hegel's: the enrichment of language. One will see the history of both the race and oneself as the development of richer, fuller ways of formulating one's desires and hopes, and thus making those desires and hopes themselves—and thereby oneself—richer and fuller. I shall call such a development the "acquisition of new vocabularies of moral reflection." By "a vocabulary of moral reflection" I mean a set of terms in which one compares oneself to other human beings. Such vocabularies contain terms like magnanimous, a true Christian, decent, cowardly, God-fearing, hypocritical, self-deceptive, epicene, self-destructive, cold, an antique Roman, a saint, a Julien Sorel, a Becky Sharpe, a red-blooded American, a shy gazelle, a hyena, depressive, a Bloomsbury type, a man of respect, a grande dame. Such terms are possible answers to the question "What is he or she like?" and thus possible answers to the question "What am *I* like?" By summing up patterns of behavior, they are tools for criticizing the character of other and for creating one's own. They are the terms one uses when one tries to resolve moral dilemmas by asking "What sort of person would I be if I did this?"

This question is, of course, not the only question one asks when reflecting about what to do. One also asks, for example, "How would I justify myself to so-and-so?" and "Would this action violate the general rule that...?" But

---

17   See Hans Blumenberg's discussion of "rhetorical curiosity," and especially his contrast between the medieval criticism of curiosity and Bacon's praise of it, in *The Legitimacy of the Modern Age,* trans. Robert Wallace (Cambridge: MIT Press, 1983).

answers to these questions will reflect the vocabulary of moral reflection at one's disposal. That vocabulary helps one decide to which sort of people to justify oneself. It puts some flesh on abstract rules like the categorical imperative and "Maximize human happiness!" It is distinctions between such vocabularies, rather than between general principles, that differentiate the moralities of communities, historical epochs, and epochs in the life of the curious intellectual. The availability of a richer vocabulary of moral deliberation is what one chiefly has in mind when one says that we are, morally speaking, more sensitive and sophisticated than our ancestors or than our younger selves.

Much could be said about how the addition of specifically psychoanalytic concepts to religious and philosophical concepts (and to the invocation of historical and literary archetypes) has influenced contemporary patterns of moral deliberation.[18] My theme, however, is different. I want to focus on the way in which Freud, by helping us see ourselves as centerless, as random assemblages of contingent and idiosyncratic needs rather than as more or less adequate exemplifications of a common human essence, opened up new possibilities for the aesthetic life. He helped us become increasingly ironic, playful, free, and inventive in our choice of self-descriptions. This has been an important factor in our ability to slough off the idea that we have a true self, one shared with all other humans, and the related notion that the demands of this true self—the specifically moral demands—take precedence over all others. It has helped us think of moral reflection and sophistication as a matter of self-creation rather than self-knowledge. Freud made the paradigm of self-knowledge the discovery of the fortuitous materials out of which we must construct ourselves rather than the discovery of the principles to which we must conform. He thus made the desire for purification seem more self-deceptive, and the quest for self-enlargement more promising.

By contrast, the history of modern philosophy has centered on attempts to preserve an enclave of nonmechanism, and thus to keep alive the notion of a "true self" and the plausibility of a morality of self-purification. Descartes was willing to follow Galileo in dissolving all the Aristotelian natural kinds into so many vortices of corpuscles, with one exception. He wanted the

---

18   See, for example, Adam Morton, "Freudian Commonsense," in *Philosophical Essays on Freud* (cited above in n. 9). I think that Morton asks just the right questions, although I have doubts about the character/personality distinction that he draws.

mind to remain exempt from this dissolution. The mind and its faculties (notably intellect, conceived of as immediate, nondiscursive grasp of truth) were to remain as Platonism and Christianity had conceived of them. This enclave of nonmechanism that Descartes claimed to have descried became the preserve of a subject called "metaphysics."[19] Kant recognized the ad hoc and factitious character of this Cartesian attempt to keep the world safe for nonmechanism, and so he developed a different, more drastic, strategy to achieve the same end. He was willing to put mind and matter on a par, and to follow Hume in dissolving what he called "the empirical self" into predictable associations of mental atoms. But he distinguished that self from the true self, the moral self, the part of the self that was an agent, rather than a subject of scientific inquiry.

This still smaller and more mysterious enclave of nonmechanism became the preserve of a subject called "moral philosophy." Kant tried to make morality a nonempirical matter, something that would never again have anything to fear from religion, science, or the arts, nor have anything to learn from them.[20] For, Kant explained, the reason why the New Science had described a world with no moral lesson, a world without a moral point, was that it described a world of appearance. By contrast, the true world was a world that was, so to speak, nothing but point: nothing but a moral imperative, nothing but a call to moral purity.

One result of Kant's initiative was to impoverish the vocabulary of moral philosophy and to turn the enrichment of our vocabulary of moral reflection over to novelists, poets, and dramatists.[21] The nineteenth-century

---

19   Consider Leibniz's novel and influential use of the terms *physics* and *metaphysics* to name the study of mechanism and of nonmechanism, respectively— to distinguish between the area in which Newton was right and the area in which Aristotle and the scholastics had been right.

20   As J. B. Schneewind has pointed out to me, this remark is accurate only for Kant's early thinking on morality. Later in his life the purity and isolation claimed for morality in the *Grundlagen* became compromised in various ways. It was, however, the early writings on morality that became associated with Kant's name, and that his successors were concerned to criticize.

21   See Iris Murdoch, *The Sovereignty of Good* (New York: Schocken Books, 1971), 58: "It is a shortcoming of much contemporary moral philosophy that it eschews discussion of the separate virtues, preferring to proceed directly to some sovereign concept such as sincerity, or authenticity, or freedom, thereby imposing, it seems to me, an unexamined and empty idea of unity, and impoverishing our moral language in an important area." Murdoch's claim that "the most essential and fundamental aspect of our culture is the study of literature, since this is an education in how

novel, in particular, filled a vacuum left by the retreat of one-half of moral philosophy into idealist metaphysics and the advance of the other half into politics.[22] Another result was what Alasdair MacIntyre calls the invention of "the individual"—a moral self who existed "prior to and apart from all roles,"[23] who was independent of any social or historical context. To say that the moral self exists apart from all roles means that it will remain the same no matter what situation it finds itself in, no matter what language it uses to create its self-image, no matter what its vocabulary of moral deliberation may be. That, in turn, means that the moral self has no need to work out a sensitive and sophisticated vocabulary as an instrument to create its character. For the only character that matters is the one it already has. Once it began to seem (as it did to Kant) that we had always known a priori all there was to know about the "morally relevant" portion of human beings, the Hegelian urge to enrich our vocabulary of moral reflection began to seem (as it did to Kierkegaard) a merely "aesthetic" demand, something that might amuse a leisured elite but which had no relevance to our moral responsibilities.[24]

This account of modern philosophy can be summarized by saying that when modern science made it hard to think of man as a natural kind, philosophy responded by inventing an unnatural kind. It was perhaps predictable that the sequence of descriptions of this self that begins with

---

to picture and understand human situations" (34) would have meant something different two hundred years ago. For then the term *literature* covered Hume's *Enquiries* and his *History* as well as novels, plays, and poems. Our modern contrast between literature and moral philosophy is one result of the development that Murdoch describes: "Philosophy...has been busy dismantling the old substantial picture of the 'self,' and ethics has not proved itself able to rethink this concept for moral purposes. Moral philosophy, and indeed morals, are thus undefended against an irresponsible and undirected self-assertion which goes easily hand-in-hand with some brand of pseudo-scientific determinism. An unexamined sense of the strength of the machine is combined with an illusion of leaping out of it. The younger Sartre, and many British moral philosophers, represent this last dry distilment of Kant's view of the world" (47–48).

22   The latter phenomenon is exemplified by, for example, Bentham and Marx—philosophers who have been responsible for much good in the public sphere but who are useless as advisers on the development of one's moral character.

23   See the passage from MacIntyre quoted in note 4 above.

24   For a contemporary account of the contrast between the Kantian and the Hegelian attitudes, see Alan Donagan, *A Theory of Morality* (Chicago: University of Chicago Press, 1977), chap. 1, on "Hegel's doctrine of the emptiness of the moral point of view" (10).

Descartes should end with Sartre: the self as a blank space in the middle of a machine—an *être-pour-soi,* a "hole in being." By contrast, Freud stands with Hegel against Kant, in an attitude of Nietzschean exuberance rather than Sartrean embarrassment. He offers us a way to reinvent the search for enlargement, and thereby reinvents the morality of character. I can summarize my account of how he does this in five points:

1. Whereas everybody from Plato to Kant had identified our central self, our conscience, the standard-setting, authoritative part of us, with universal truths, general principles, and a common human nature, Freud made conscience just one more, not particularly central, part of a larger, homogenous machine. He identified the sense of duty with the internalization of a host of idiosyncratic, accidental episodes. On his account our sense of moral obligation is not a matter of general ideas contemplated by the intellect, but rather of traces of encounters between particular people and our bodily organs. He saw the voice of conscience not as the voice of the part of the soul that deals with generalities as opposed to the part that deals with particulars, but rather as the (usually distorted) memory of certain very particular events.

2. This identification did not take the form of a reductive claim that morality was "nothing but..." delayed responses to forgotten stimuli. Since Freud was willing to view *every* part of life, every human activity, in the same terms, there was no contrast to be drawn between the "merely" mechanical and reactive character of moral experience and the free and spontaneous character of something else (e.g., science, art, philosophy or psychoanalytic theory).

3. Nor did this identification of conscience with memory of idiosyncratic events take the form of the claim that talk about such events was a ("scientific") substitute for moral deliberation. Freud did not suggest that we would see ourselves more clearly, or choose more wisely, by restricting our vocabulary of moral reflection to psychoanalytic terms. On the contrary, Freud dropped the Platonic metaphor of "seeing ourselves more clearly" in favor of the Baconian idea of theory as a tool for bringing about desirable change.[25] He was far from thinking that psychoanalytic theory was the *only*

---

25   Rieff makes this contrast between Platonic and Baconian attitudes, saying that the latter, the "second theory of theory," views theory as "arming us with the weapons for transforming reality instead of forcing us to conform to it. Psychoanalytic theory belongs to the second tradition" (*The Triumph of the Therapeutic,* 55–56). This view of Freud's aim is central to my account of his achievement, and I am much indebted

tool needed for self-enlargement.

4. This Baconian attitude was the culmination of the mechanizing movement that had begun in the seventeenth century. That movement had replaced the attempt to contemplate the essences of natural kinds with the attempt to tinker with the machines that compose the world. But not until Freud did we get a usable way of thinking of *ourselves* as machines to be tinkered with, a self-image that enabled us to weave terms describing psychic mechanisms into our strategies of character-formation.

5. The increased ability of the syncretic, ironic, nominalist intellectual to move back and forth between, for example, religious, moral, scientific, literary, philosophical, and psychoanalytical vocabularies without asking the question "And which of these shows us how things *really* are?"—the intellectual's increased ability to treat vocabularies as tools rather than mirrors—is Freud's major legacy. He broke some of the last chains that bind us to the Greek idea that we, or the world, have a nature that, once discovered, will tell us what we should do with ourselves. He made it far more difficult than it was before to ask the question "Which is my true self?" or "What is human nature?" By letting us see that even in the enclave which philosophy had fenced off, there was nothing to be found save traces of accidental encounters, he left us able to tolerate the ambiguities that the religious and philosophical traditions had hoped to eliminate.

"The Rich Aesthete, the Manager, and the Therapist"

My account of Freud as a Baconian has taken for granted that the move from Aristotelian to Baconian views of the nature of knowledge, like that from an ethics of purity to one of self-enrichment, was desirable. My enthusiasm for the mechanization and decentering of the world is dictated by my assumption that the ironic, playful intellectual is a desirable character-type, and that Freud's importance lies in his contribution to the formation of such a character. These assumptions are challenged by those who see the mechanization of nature as a prelude to barbarism. Such critics emphasize, as I have, the link between a pragmatic, tinkering approach to nature and the self, and the aesthetic search for novel experiences and novel language. But they condemn both.

The most thoroughly thought-out, if most abstract, account of the

_____

to Rieff's work.

relation between technology and aestheticism is offered by Heidegger.[26] But the more concrete criticisms of modern ways of thinking offered by Alasdair MacIntyre in *After Virtue* are more immediately relevant to the topics I have been discussing. MacIntyre would agree, more or less, with my description of the connections between Baconian ways of thought and Nietzschean values. But he takes the fact that the paradigmatic character-types of modernity are "the Rich Aesthete, the Manager, and the Therapist" (29) to show that these ways of thought, and these values, are undesirable. In MacIntyre's view, the abandonment of an Aristotelian "functional concept of man" leads to "emotivism"—the obliteration of any genuine distinction between manipulative and non-manipulative social relations" (22).

MacIntyre is, I think, right in saying that contemporary moral discourse is a confusing and inconsistent blend of notions that make sense only in an Aristotelian view of the world (e.g., "reason," "human nature," "natural rights") with mechanistic, anti-Aristotelian notions that implicitly repudiate such a view. But whereas MacIntyre thinks we need to bring back Aristotelian ways of thinking to make our moral discourse coherent, I think we should do the opposite and make the discourse coherent by discarding the last vestiges of those ways of thinking.[27] I would welcome a culture dominated by "the Rich Aesthete, the Manager, and the Therapist" so long as *everybody* who wants to gets to be an aesthete (and, if not rich, as comfortably off as most—as rich as the Managers can manage, guided by Rawls's Difference Principle).

---

26   See [Martin] Heidegger's essays "The Question Concerning Technology" and "The Age of the World Picture" in *The Question Concerning Technology and Other Essays,* trans. W. Lovitt (New York: Harper and Row, 1977). I suggest a Deweyan response to Heidegger's view of technology at the end of "Heidegger, Contingency, and Pragmatism" [in Rorty, *Essays on Heidegger and Others: Philosophical Papers Volume 2* (Cambridge: Cambridge University Press, 1991), 29–49]. MacIntyre would join me in repudiating Heidegger's attack on technology but would retain Heidegger's account of the shift in moral consciousness that followed upon the abandonment of an Aristotelian world view.

27   It is tempting to say that I would accept MacIntyre's claim that the only real choice is between Aristotle and Nietzsche, and then side with Nietzsche. But the choice is too dramatic and too simple. By the time MacIntyre gets rid of the nonsense in Aristotle (e.g., what he calls the "metaphysical biology"), Aristotle does not look much like himself. By the time I would finish discarding the bits of Nietzsche I do not want (e.g., his lapses into metaphysical biology, his distrust of Hegel, his *ressentiment,* etc.) he would not look much like Nietzsche. The opposition between these two ideal types is useful only if one does not press it too hard.

Further, I think that we can live with the Freudian thought that every-thing everybody does to everyone else (even those they love blindly and helplessly) can be described, for therapeutic or other purposes, as manip-ulation. The postulation of unintrospectible systems of beliefs and desires ensures that there will be a coherent and informative narrative to be told in those terms, one that will interpret all personal and social relations, even the tenderest and most sacred, in terms of "making use of" others. Once those extra persons who explain akrasia and other forms of irratio-nality are taken into account, there are, so to speak, too many selves for "selflessness" to seem a useful notion. But the increased ability to explain, given by Freud's postulation of additional persons, hardly prevents us from drawing the common-sense distinction between manipulating people (i.e., consciously, and deceptively, employing them as instruments for one's own purposes) and not manipulating them. The availability of a description for explanatory purposes does not entail its use in moral reflection, any more than it precludes it.

MacIntyre construes "emotivism" as the only option left, once one abandons the Aristotelian idea of man, because he retains a pre-Freudian[28] division of human faculties. In terms of this division, "desire" or "will" or "passion" represents the only alternative to "reason" (construed as a faculty of seeing things as they are in themselves). But dividing people up this way begs the question against other ways of describing them—for example, Freud's way. Freud (at least according to the Davidsonian interpretation I have developed here) drops the whole idea of "faculties," and substitutes the notion of a plurality of sets of beliefs and desires. MacIntyre's defini-tion of "emotivism" ("the doctrine that all evaluative judgments and more specifically all moral judgments are *nothing but* expressions of preference, expressions of attitude or feeling" [11]) makes sense only if there is some-thing else such judgments might have been—for example, expressions of a correct "rational" grasp of the nature of the human being.

Moral psychology, like moral discourse, is at present an incoherent blend of Aristotelian and mechanist ways of speaking. I would urge that if we eradicate the former, "emotivism" will no longer be an intelligible posi-tion. More generally, if we take Freud to heart, we shall not have to choose between an Aristotelian "functional" concept of humanity, one that will

---

28   Or, more generally, premechanist (and thus pre-Humean: see note 10 on Hume and faculty psychology).

provide moral guidance, and Sartrean "dreadful freedom." For the Sartrean conception of the self as pure freedom will be seen as merely the last gasp of the Aristotelian tradition—a self-erasing expression of the Cartesian determination to find *something* nonmechanical at the center of the machine, if only a "hole in being."[29] We shall not need a picture of "the human self" in order to have morality—neither of a nonmechanical enclave nor of a meaningless void where such an enclave ought to have been.

It seems a point in my favor that MacIntyre does not answer the question of whether it is "rationally justifiable [*pace* Sartre] to conceive of each human life as a unity" (189) by saying (with Aristotle) "yes, because the function of man is…." Rather, he offers us "a concept of a self whose unity resides in the unity of a narrative which links birth to life to death as narrative beginning to middle to end" (191).[30] MacIntyre tacitly drops the Aristotelian demand that the themes of each such narrative be roughly the same for each member of a given species, and that they stay roughly constant throughout the history of the species. He seems content to urge that in order for us to exhibit the virtue of "integrity or constancy" we must see our lives in such narrative terms. To attempt that virtue is just what I have been calling "the search for perfection," and I agree that this search requires the construction of such narratives. But if we do drop the Aristotelian demand, contenting ourselves with narratives tailored ad hoc to the contingencies of individual lives, then we may welcome a Baconian culture dominated by

29 Metaphysicians like Sartre would, to paraphrase Nietzsche, rather have a metaphysics of nothingness than no metaphysics. This was a trap around which Heidegger circled in his early work but eventually walked away from, leaving Sartre to take the plunge.

30 There seems to be a tension in MacIntyre's *After Virtue* between the early chapters, in which it is suggested that unless we can identify a telos common to all members of our species we are driven to the "emotivist" view that "all moral judgments are *nothing but* expressions of preference" (11), and chapters 4–15. In the latter chapters, which MacIntyre thinks of as a rehabilitation of Aristotelianism (see 239), nothing is done to defeat the suggestion that all moral judgments are nothing but choices among competing narratives, a suggestion that is compatible with the three paradigmatically Aristotelian doctrines that MacIntyre lists on pages 183–186 of his book. By dropping what he calls "Aristotle's metaphysical biology" (183), MacIntyre also drops the attempt to evaluate "the claims to objectivity and authority" of "the lost morality of the past" (21). For unless a knowledge of the function of the human species takes us beyond MacIntyre's Socratic claim that "the good life for man is the life spent in seeking for the good life for man" (204), the idea of one narrative being more "objective and authoritative" than another, as opposed to being more detailed and inclusive, goes by the board.

"the Rich Aesthete, the Manager, and the Therapist"—not necessarily as the final goal of human progress, but at least as a considerable improvement on cultures dominated by, for example, the Warrior or the Priest.

On my account of Freud, his work enables us to construct richer and more plausible narratives of this ad hoc sort—more plausible because they will cover *all* the actions one performs in the course of one's life, even the silly, cruel, and self-destructive actions. More generally, Freud helped us see that the attempt to put together such a narrative—one that minimizes neither the contingency nor the decisive importance of the input into the machine that each of us is—must take the place of an attempt to find the function common to all such machines. If one takes Freud's advice, one finds psychological narratives without heroes or heroines. For neither Sartrean freedom, nor the will, nor the instincts, nor an internalization of a culture, nor anything else will play the role of "the true self." Instead, one tells the story of the whole machine *as* machine, without choosing a particular set of springs and wheels as protagonist. Such a story can help us, if anything can, stop the pendulum from swinging between Aristotelian attempts to discover our essence and Sartrean attempts at self-creation *de novo*.

This suggestion that our stories about ourselves must be stories of centerless mechanisms—of the determined processing of contingent input—will seem to strip us of human dignity only if we think we need *reasons* to live romantically, or to treat others decently, or to be treated decently ourselves. Questions like "Why should I hope?" or "Why should I not use others as means?" or "Why should my torturers not use me as a means?" are questions that can *only* be answered by philosophical metanarratives that tell us about a nonmechanical world and a nonmechanical self—about a world and a self that have centers, centers that are sources of authority. Such questions are tailored to fit such answers. So if we renounce such answers, such metanarratives, and fall back on narratives about the actual and possible lives of individuals, we shall have to renounce the needs that metaphysics and moral philosophy attempted to satisfy. We shall have to confine ourselves to questions like, "If I do this rather than that now, what story will I tell myself later?" We shall have to abjure questions like, "Is there something deep inside my torturer—his rationality—to which I can appeal?"

The philosophical tradition suggests that there is, indeed, something of this sort. It tends to take for granted that our dignity depends on the existence of something that can be opposed to "arbitrary will." This thing, usually called "reason," is needed to give "authority" to the first premises of our practical syllogisms. Such a view of human dignity is precisely what Freud called "the pious view of the Universe." He thought that the traditional oppositions between reason, will, and emotion—the oppositions in terms of which MacIntyre constructs his history of ethics—should be discarded in favor of distinctions between various regions of a homogenous mechanism, regions that embody a plurality of persons (that is, of incompatible systems of belief and desire). So the only version of human dignity that Freud lets us preserve is the one MacIntyre himself offers: the ability of each of us to tailor a coherent self-image for ourselves and then use it to tinker with our behavior. This ability replaces the traditional philosophical project of finding a coherent self-image that will fit the entire species to which we belong.

Given this revisionary account of human dignity, what becomes of human solidarity? In my view, Freud does nothing for either liberal or radical policies, except perhaps to supply new terms of opprobrium with which to stigmatize tyrants and torturers.[31] On the contrary, he diminishes our ability to take seriously much of the traditional jargon of both liberalism and radicalism—notions such as "human rights" and "autonomy" and slogans such as "man will prevail" and "trust the instincts of the masses." For these notions and slogans are bound up with Aristotelian attempts to find a center for the self.

On the other hand, Freud does nothing to diminish a sense of human solidarity that, rather than encompassing the entire species, restricts itself to such particular communal movements as modern science, bourgeois liberalism, or the European novel. If we avoid describing these movements in terms of metaphysical notions like "the search for truth," or "the realization of human freedom," or "the attainment of self-consciousness," histories of them will nevertheless remain available as larger narratives within which to place the narratives of our individual lives. Freud banishes philosophical

---

31   But diagnoses of the Freudian mechanisms that produce suitable candidates for the KGB and the Gestapo, of the sort made popular by Adorno and others who talk about "authoritarian personalities," add little to the familiar pre-Freudian suggestion that we might have fewer bully boys to cope with if people had more education, leisure, and money. The Adorno-Horkheimer suggestion that the rise of Nazism within a highly developed and cultivated nation shows that this familiar liberal solution is inadequate seems to me unconvincing. At any rate, it seems safe to say that Freudo-Marxist analyses of "authoritarianism" have offered no better suggestions about how to keep the thugs from taking over.

metanarratives, but he has nothing against ordinary historical narratives. Such narratives tell, for example, how we got from Galileo to Gell-Mann, or from institutions that defended merchants against feudal overlords to institutions that defend labor against capital, or from *Don Quixote* to *Pale Fire*.

Letting us see the narratives of our own lives as episodes within such larger historical narratives is, I think, as much as the intellectuals are able to do in aid of morality. The attempt of religion and metaphysics to do more—to supply a backup for moral intuitions by providing them with ahistorical "authority"—will always be self-defeating. For (given the present rate of social change) another century's worth of history will always make the last century's attempt to be ahistorical look ridiculous. The only result of such attempts is to keep the pendulum swinging between moral dogmatism and moral skepticism.[32] What metaphysics could not do, psychology, even very "deep" psychology, is not going to do either; we pick up Freud by the wrong handle if we try to find an account of "moral motivation" that is more than a reference to the historical contingencies that shaped the process of acculturation in our region and epoch.

Historical narratives about social and intellectual movements are the best tools to use in tinkering with ourselves, for such narratives suggest vocabularies of moral deliberation in which to spin coherent narratives about our individual lives. By contrast, the vocabulary Freud himself used in much of his writing—an individualist, Stoic vocabulary, charged with ironic resignation—does little for the latter purpose. It has too much in common with the vocabulary of the self-erasing narratives of Rameau's nephew, Dostoevsky's "Underground Man," and Sartre's Roquentin: stories about machines chewing themselves to pieces. By contrast, narratives that help one identify oneself with communal movements engender a sense of being a machine geared into a larger machine. This is a sense worth having. For it helps reconcile an existentialist sense of contingency and mortality with a Romantic sense of grandeur. It helps us realize that the best way of tinkering with ourselves is to tinker with something else—a mechanist way of saying that only he who loses his soul will save it.[33]

---

32 For a discussion of the causes and effects of such pendulum swings, see Annette Baier, "Doing without Moral Theory?" in her *Postures of the Mind* (Minneapolis: University of Minnesota Press, 1985).

33 This paper owes a great deal to the comments of J. B. Schneewind, Alexander Nehamas, and the late Irvin Ehrenpreis on a draft version.

CPSIA information can be obtained
at www.ICGtesting.com
Printed in the USA
LVHW040437190723
752850LV00030B/428